General Editor: Simon Trussler

Associate Editor: Malcolm Page

A Methuen Drama Book
First published in 1991 as a paperback original
by Methuen Drama, Michelin House,
81 Fulham Road, London SW3 6RB,
and HEB Inc., 361 Hanover Street,
Portsmouth, New Hampshire 03801, USA

Typeset in 9/10 Times by
L. Anderson Typesetting,
Woodchurch, Kent TN26 3TB

Printed in Great Britain
by Cox and Wyman Ltd.,
Cardiff Road, Reading

ISBN 413 62890 6

British Library Cataloguing in Publication Data
is available from the British Library

Contents

Acknowledgements

We should like to thank the following for their
assistance during our research:

Howard Rosenstone and Renata Cobbs, Rosenstone/Wender,
New York; Becky Browder, Lincoln Center, New York;
Yolanda Lyon-Miller, Theatre Department, Roosevelt
University, Chicago; Lauren Bufferd, Special Collections,
Chicago Public Library; Pauline Ryall, Goldsmiths' College
Library, University of London; Betty L. Corwin, TOFT
Collection, New York Public Library at Lincoln Center;
Celia Morgan, Press Office, Royal National Theatre;
translators: Valentina Giambianco, John Gribbin,
Marc von Henning, Yukiko Itoh; typists: Brenda Ford,
Marlene Miller; facilitators: Blake Hambrick,
Kim Perseke; special enquiries: Philip Dykes,
Selda Ergün, Dominic Jones; Catherine Shaddix,
Mamet's personal assistant; J. J. Johnston, Susan Nussbaum,
and Mamet's associates who gave us interviews:

Joe Mantegna at the Organic Theater, Chicago,
28 May 1989; Gregory Mosher at the Vivian Beaumont
Theater, Lincoln Center, New York, 8 June 1989;
Colin Stinton at the Royal National Theatre, London,
27 July 1989; Jack Shepherd at Goldsmiths' College,
University of London, 12 October 1989; John Dillon
at the Milwaukee Repertory Theater, 10 November 1989;
W. H. Macy at the Mitzi E. Newhouse Theater,
Lincoln Center, New York, 28 December 1990;
and Bill Bryden at the Royal National Theatre, London,
5 January 1990.

Finally, our thanks to David Mamet, for his generosity
in showing us unpublished materials, and for taking
the time to talk to us in Cambridge, Massachusetts,
in June 1989

The theatre is, by its nature, an ephemeral art: yet it is a daunting task to track down the newspaper reviews, or contemporary statements from the writer or his director, which are often all that remain to help us recreate some sense of what a particular production was like. This series is therefore intended to make readily available a selection of the comments that the critics made about the plays of leading modern dramatists at the time of their production — and to trace, too, the course of each writer's own views about his work and his world.

In addition to combining a uniquely convenient source of such elusive *documentation*, the 'Writer-Files' series also assembles the *information* necessary for readers to pursue further their interest in a particular writer or work. Variations in quantity between one writer's output and another's, differences in temperament which make some readier than others to talk about their work, and the variety of critical response, all mean that the presentation and balance of material shifts between one volume and another: but we have tried to arrive at a format for the series which will nevertheless enable users of one volume readily to find their way around any other.

Section 1, 'A Brief Chronology', provides a quick conspective overview of each playwright's life and career. *Section 2* deals with the plays themselves, arranged chronologically in the order of their composition: information on first performances, major revivals, and publication is followed by a brief synopsis (for quick reference set in slightly larger, italic type), then by a representative selection of the critical response, and of the dramatist's own comments on the play and its theme.

Section 3 offers concise guidance to each writer's work in non-dramatic forms, while *Section 4*, 'The Writer on His Work', brings together comments from the playwright himself on more general matters of construction, opinion, and artistic development. Finally, *Section 5* provides a bibliographical guide to other primary and secondary sources of further reading, among which full details will be found of works cited elsewhere under short titles, and of collected editions of the plays — but not of individual titles, particulars of which will be found with the other factual data in Section 2.

The 'Writer-Files' hope by striking this kind of balance between information and a wide range of opinion to offer 'companions' to the study of major playwrights in the modern repertoire — not in that dangerous pre-digested fashion which can too readily quench the desire to read the plays themselves, nor so prescriptively as to allow any single line of approach to predominate, but rather to encourage readers to form their own judgements of the plays in a wide-ranging context.

David Mamet is the latest in a line of American exponents of poetic realism which stretches from the late O'Neill through the early Williams and Miller to the middle (some would say middling) Albee. But Mamet is also very much his own man, for whom *being* a man in the late twentieth century presents special challenges and problems. Among his strengths are an assurance in the vernacular which embraces the full vocabulary of obscenity, and an ability to compel attention to a stage rarely peopled by more than a handful of characters — while he is at his least assured (certainly his least characteristic) in a work like *Edmond*, where precision gives way before the vagaries of impressionism.

At a time when, properly, many male dramatists are concerned to recognize the insights of feminism, Mamet is unusual in his complementary rather than contradictory concern with the significance of male bonding, whether at the individual level, in the petty complicities of *Glengarry Glen Ross*, or in the wider implications of what that play's first director, Bill Bryden, describes on page 60 as 'a way of explaining Nixon's America through seven of its citizens'. Such an explanation must necessarily acknowledge that language conceals as much as it reveals: and the playing of Mamet's subtext through physicality and gestic nuance has been greatly assisted by his long association with a group of performers and directors of like sensibility. Their names frequently recur in the credits recorded in this *Writer-File*: and it is thus particularly helpful that its compilers have been able to interview many members of this group (as well as those responsible for introducing Mamet to British audiences), and to set their views of the plays alongside those of the dramatist and the critics. For Mamet's work, like Shakespeare's, contains few stage directions: like Shakespeare, he is confident that close colleagues will *know* what to do in performance — or that others, less familiar, will accept that it is part of their expected expertise to find out.

If Mamet thus writes with a sure feeling for theatricality, he also writes *about* theatricality, whether overtly, as the very title of *A Life in the Theatre* anticipates, or in implicit awareness of the importance of role-playing in a society where to reveal one's selfhood at best seems to acknowledge weakness, at worst invites betrayal. His characters teeter between the desire for self-revelation and the compulsion to conceal, fulfilling their need for communality in the small rituals through which its semblance is achieved in a society divided into winners and losers.

Simon Trussler

1947   30 Nov., born David Alan Mamet, son of Bernard, a labour lawyer, and Lenora, a teacher. Early life spent in Flossmoor, a suburb south of Chicago, with his parents and younger sister Lyn.

1957   Attends Rich Central High School. Parents separate and divorce a year later. Lives with his mother and sister in South Shore; later moves to the 'model suburb' of Olympia Fields.

1963-65   Mamet lives with his father in the Lincoln Park area of Chicago. Attends Francis Parker Private School. Works as a 'busboy' (kitchen porter) at 'Second City', which performed its first revue at the Wells Street venue in Dec. 1959, with Paul Sills as founding artistic director. Mamet also works backstage at Hull House Theater, established by William (Bob) Sickinger in Nov. 1963. Productions include plays by Pinter, Brecht, and Albee. Mike Nussbaum is an early company member.

1965-69   Attends Goddard College, Plainfield, Vermont, to study for his BA in English Literature. Spends one summer vacation working as a dancer with Maurice Chevalier's company in Montreal, Canada. His father arranges vacation work for him as a steward on a cargo boat on Lake Michigan.

1967-68   Spends Goddard's 'Junior Year Abroad' studying acting under Sanford Meisner at the Neighborhood Playhouse, New York.

1969   Graduates from Goddard. His thesis paper is a 'Second City'-style revue called *Camel*. Joins a professional theatre company based at McGill University, Toronto. Performs in Pinter's *The Homecoming*. Works in variety of theatre jobs, including stage-managing the long-running off-Broadway hit *The Fantastiks*. In Chicago the Goodman Theater separates from its parent organization, the Chicago Art Institute, and establishes a permanent professional company. The Body Politic opens on Lincoln Avenue as a home for avant-garde, experimental drama. Paul Sills is appointed artistic director.

1970   Mamet spends summer working in a real-estate office on the North Side of Chicago. Sept., takes up position as Acting Instructor at Marlboro College, Vermont. Directs his students in an early version of *Lakeboat*. Stuart Gordon brings his Organic Theater troupe to Chicago, and moves into Body Politic venue. Joe Mantegna joins company.

1971 Mamet works for a year as an Acting Instructor at Goddard College, Vermont. Forms the St. Nicholas Theater Company with two students, William H. Macy and Steven Schachter. Group performs first drafts of *Duck Variations* and *Sexual Perversity in Chicago*. Also produced is a slapstick send-up of old Indian legends entitled *Lone Canoe*.

1972 Summer, *Duck Variations* and *Sexual Perversity in Chicago* are produced by the company in a small venue in Boston ('about seven people saw them', according to W. H. Macy). Mamet returns to Chicago. Macy and Schachter move to Los Angeles. Autumn, *Duck Variations*, in a double-bill with the monologue *Litko*, is performed in the 'New Room' of the Body Politic Theater.

1973 Mamet plays a small part in Body Politic's production of *The Night They Shot Harry Lindsey with a 155mm Howitzer and Blamed it on Zebras*. Shows script of *Sexual Perversity* to director, Stuart Gordon, and the two begin to rework it for a new production. Works with a children's theatre company, where he meets J. J. Johnston.

1974 June, Organic Theater presents *Sexual Perversity in Chicago* at the Leo Lerner Theater. Mamet reforms St. Nicholas Theater Company in Chicago with Macy, Schachter, Patricia Cox (a graduate of the University of Chicago), and local musician Alaric 'Rokko' Jans. 3 Oct., first production is the premiere of *Squirrels*. Company also performs *Mackinac* — a play for children about Indians in North Michigan — at the Bernard Horwich Jewish Community Center. *Sexual Perversity* wins Jefferson Award for Best New Chicago Play. Mamet is also a faculty member, Illinois Arts Council. 'Off-Loop' theatre community firmly established with founding of Wisdom Bridge, Victory Gardens, and North Light Repertory theatres. Gregory Mosher, young graduate of the Juilliard School, New York, is appointed as assistant to the artistic director of the Goodman Theater.

1975 Feb., Mamet directs his adaptation of Eugene O'Neill's early play *Beyond the Horizon* (1918) for St Nicholas at the Grace Lutheran Church, West Baldwin Street (according to Mamet, 'Everyone hated it!'). The St. Nicholas season continues with Shakespeare's *A Midsummer Night's Dream*; a version of Chaucer's *Canterbury Tales*; and, in June, their first popular success, *The Poet and the Rent*. For much of the season, the company performs *The Dream* as a matinee, *The Tales* in the evening, and *The Poet*, a children's play, at midnight, each in a different venue. 23 Oct., Gregory Mosher directs the premiere of *American Buffalo* at the Ruth Page Auditorium as part of the Goodman Theater's Stage Two season of new plays; the cast includes Macy and Johnston. Nov., Bernard Horwich Center hosts St. Nicholas's production of *Marranos* (*Swine*) — a play about the persecution of Jews during the Spanish Inquisition. Dec., *Sexual Perversity in Chicago* opens off-off-Broadway, in a double-bill with *Duck Variations*, in the St. Clement's Theater, New York, after an earlier show-case production of *Duck Variations* is cancelled due to an Equity union dispute. *Sexual Perversity* is awarded an Obie for Best Play. St. Nicholas moves into its permanent home on Halsted Street. Season opens with transfer of *American Buffalo* from the Goodman Stage Two. Mike Nussbaum joins the cast. Continues with Miller's *A View From the Bridge* and premiere of Julian Barry's *Sitcom*. St. Nicholas also organizes classes in acting technique, based on the methods of Sanford Meisner, taught by Mamet and company members. By 1977, these classes develop into a full training programme for actors, designers, directors, and stage managers. The St. Nicholas Theatre, at its height, has a school with 1,200 students and a production budget nearing $1 million. Mamet also Contributing Editor of *Oui* Magazine, and Visiting Lecturer at University of Chicago, an appointment which continues through to following year.

1976   7 and 8 Jan., *Squirrels* is revived by St. Nicholas for two benefit performances. 9 Jan., *Reunion* (written in 1973) is presented in a midnight 'showcase'. 23 Jan., *American Buffalo* opens at the St. Clements Theater, New York. Mamet resigns the artistic directorship of the St. Nicholas Company over a dispute about the production of *Sitcom*. Moves to New York. 16 June, *Sexual Perversity in Chicago* and *Duck Variations* open off-Broadway at the Cherry Lane Theater, New York. The double-bill runs for 273 performances. *Buffalo* wins a Jefferson Award for its Chicago run and an Obie in New York. Mamet awarded New York State Council of the Arts Grant and a Rockefeller award, also receiving a CBS Fellowship in Creative Writing, which involves lecturing part-time at Yale University. Steppenwolf Theatre Company formed in Chicago.

1977   3 Feb., Goodman Stage Two presents *A Life in the Theatre*, with Joe Mantegna joining the Mamet regulars. 16 Feb., *American Buffalo* opens on Broadway at the Barrymore Theater. It runs for 135 performances and is awarded the New York Drama Critics' Circle Award. Feb., *All Men Are Whores* performed at the Yale Cabaret Theatre. 11 May, St. Nicholas premieres *The Water Engine*. June, *The Revenge of the Space Pandas, or Binky Rudich and the Two-Speed*

Clock is performed by the St. Clements Stage Company. 14 Oct., *Reunion* is presented in a double-bill with premiere of *Dark Pony* at the Yale Repertory Theater, New Haven. 20 Oct., *A Life in the Theatre* opens in New York at the Theatre de Lys. Runs for 288 performances. 11 Nov., *The Woods* directed by Mamet at St. Nicholas. *Revenge of the Space Pandas* revived by St. Nicholas. 1 Dec., *Sexual Perversity in Chicago* and *Duck Variations* open at the Regent Theatre, London — the first performance of Mamet's work abroad. Show runs for six weeks. 20 Dec., Mamet marries Lindsay Crouse, the actress.

1978 5 Jan., Joseph Papp produces *The Water Engine* in New York at his Shakespeare Festival Public Theater. Feb., Second City's annual revue is entitled *Sexual Perversity among the Buffalo* and includes an affectionate parody of Mamet's style. 6 Mar., *The Water Engine* transfers to Broadway's Plymouth Theatre, with *Mr. Happiness* included as a prologue, but runs for only 16 performances. 22 Mar., Gregory Mosher, the new Artistic Director of the Goodman Theater, appoints Mamet as Associate Artistic Director and Writer-in-Residence. 28 June, *American Buffalo* has its European premiere at the National Theatre, London.

1979 16 Jan., *A Sermon* is performed as part of a double-bill with *Sexual Perversity* at the newly opened Apollo Theater, Chicago. Feb., Mamet directs *The Blue Hour* at Papp's Public Theater, New York. 25 Apr., *The Woods* opens in New York. Closes after just 33 performances. 24 May, a new play under an old title, *Lone Canoe* receives a disastrous premiere at the Goodman in front of an audience comprising the American Theatre Critics Association, which was holding its annual convention in Chicago. In New York, *The Poet and the Rent* plays at the Circle in the Square Repertory Theater. 27 June, the Theatre de Lys production of *A Life in the Theatre* is broadcast nationally on Public Television (PBS). 18 July, British premiere of the play at the Open Space, London. 18 Oct., Mamet directs a triple bill of *Reunion*, *Dark Pony*, and *The Sanctity of Marriage* at the Circle in the Square, New York. 14 Dec., the short sketch *Shoeshine* is presented at the Ensemble Studio Theatre, New York.

1980 Apr., Milwaukee Repertory Theater produces a revised version of *Lakeboat*. Oct., Long Wharf Theater, New Haven, revives *American Buffalo* with Al Pacino. 2 Dec., Mamet directs *Twelfth Night* for the Yale Repertory Theater.

1981 Apr., the film *The Postman Always Rings Twice* — Mamet's first screenplay — is released. June, Long Wharf *American Buffalo* produced off-Broadway at the Circle in the Square. St. Nicholas Theater closes: the venue becomes home to Steppenwolf.

1982 17 May, rehearsed reading of the children's play *The Frog Prince* at the Goodman. Mamet redirects *The Woods* with the original Chicago cast in New York. Again the play is poorly received. 4 June, Goodman premieres *Edmond*. 27 Oct., *Edmond* reaches New York and wins an Obie, but runs for only 77 performances. Dec., the film *The Verdict* is released. Mamet's screenplay is nominated for an Academy Award for Best Adaptation.

1983 2 May, the Goodman main stage produces Mamet's adaptation of *Red River* by Pierre Laville. 6 May, five sketches under the collective title of *Five Unrelated Pieces* are presented in the New York Ensemble Theater's Marathon Festival of One-Act Plays. 3 June, *The Disappearance of the Jews* is presented in a triple-bill at the Goodman Studio with Elaine May's *Hotline* and Shel Silverstein's *Gorilla*. 14 July, the sketches *The Dog*, *Film Crew*, and *Four AM* appear as part of 'Three by Three', a collection of work by Mamet, Silverstein, and Neil Cuthbert, at 'Jason's' in the Park Royal Hotel, New York. 21 Sept., the world premiere of *Glengarry Glen Ross* takes place at the National Theatre, London; wins the Society of West End Theatre Award for best new play. Oct., Long Wharf production of *American Buffalo* reaches Broadway; Al Pacino is joined by J. J. Johnston, returning to his original role.

1984 6 Feb., *Glengarry Glen Ross* has its American premiere at the Goodman. 25 Mar., the production moves to Broadway's John Golden Theater, where it runs for 378 performances. 16 Apr., Mamet is awarded the Pulitzer Prize for *Glengarry*. 24 May, *Vermont Sketches* feature in the Ensemble Studio Theater's second Marathon Festival of One-Act Plays. Aug., Long Wharf's *American Buffalo* plays at the Duke of York's Theatre, London. Gregory Mosher announces the creation of the New Theater Company, formed by the Chicago Theater Group, the parent organization of the Goodman — an independent company with its own venue. The project is the brain child of Mosher and Mamet, and includes many of the regular actors from past collaborations — Nussbaum, Macy, and Crouse among them.

1985 4 Mar., *Goldberg Street* and *Cross Patch* are broadcast on WNU Radio, Chicago, featuring members of the New Theater Company. 14 Mar., New Theater opens its season with Mamet's adaptation of *The Cherry Orchard*, performed in the Goodman Studio. 24 Mar., *South Bank Show* programme entitled 'David Mamet, Playwright' broadcast

11

by London Weekend Television. 19 Apr., the New Theater Company moves into its new venue, the Briar Street Theater, with *The Shawl* and *The Spanish Prisoner*. Sept., Mamet contributes *Vint* to the American Repertory Theater Company's touring production of *Orchards* — a programme of sketches by contemporary playwrights based on short stories by Anton Chekhov. Gregory Mosher is appointed Artistic Director of the Lincoln Center Theater, New York. 24 Dec., his first production is a double-bill of *The Shawl* and *Prairie du Chien*. The film *About Last Night* — loosely based on *Sexual Perversity in Chicago* — is released. European premiere of *Edmond* at the Newcastle Playhouse, a co-production between the Tyne-Wear Company and the Royal Court Theatre, London. 3 Dec., *Edmond* opens at the Royal Court.

1986 June, the film *The Untouchables,* with screenplay by Mamet, is released. A collection of Mamet's essays entitled *Writing in Restaurants* is published. Mamet and Macy hold classes in acting for students of New York University at Mamet's home in Vermont. These classes become the 'Practical Aesthetics Workshop' (PAW) and the basis of *The Practical Handbook for the Actor*. Out of the PAW is formed the Atlantic Theatre Company. Mamet plays a small cameo role in the film *Black Widow*, directed by Bob Rafelson, which is released in Feb. the following year.

1987 13 Jan., NBC broadcasts 'Wasted Weekend', an episode written by Mamet for the television series *Hill Street Blues*. Oct., Mamet's first film as writer-director, *House of Games*, is chosen to close the New York Film Festival. 'Mamet: Profile of a Writer', video cassette of *South Bank Show* programme, released.

1988 10 Feb., Mamet delivers the Theodore Spencer Memorial Lecture at the Loeb Drama Center, Harvard University; his subject is 'Decay'. Mar., Mamet's second film as writer-director, *Things Change*, is chosen to open the London Film Festival; released in America later in the year. 16 Apr., New Theater Company presents *Uncle Vanya* at the American Repertory Theater, Cambridge, Mass. 3 May, *Speed-The-Plow* opens on Broadway at the Royale Theater. 12 May, John Tillinger directs the 20-minute sketch *Where Were You When It Went Down?* as part of the off-Broadway revue *Urban Blight*. 11 Oct., Mamet directs *Sketches of War* at the Colonial Theater, Boston. The programme, featuring Don Ameche, Michael J. Fox, Al Pacino, Donald Sutherland, Christopher Walken, and Lindsay Crouse, is a benefit for homeless Vietnam veterans in the Boston area; the sketches include pieces by Shakespeare, David Rabe, and Mamet's *Cross Patch*. 19 Oct., Mamet and his partner Michael Hausman are executive producers of *Lip*

Service written by Howard Korder, broadcast by HBO Television. Mamet declined to direct the project in favour of W. H. Macy. *Warm and Cold* published, dedicated to his two daughters, Frances and Willa.

1989   25 Jan., *Speed-The-Plow* opens at the Royal National Theatre, London. Feb., a passage from *Dodge* is published in *Harper's Magazine* together with extracts from the work of David Hare and Harold Pinter. 23 Aug., reading of *Bobby Gould in Hell* (as work in progress) followed by Mamet in conversation with Mosher at the Royal National Theatre, London. 29 Aug., British premiere of *The Water Engine* at Hampstead Theatre Club, London. 31 Oct., major revival of *A Life in the Theatre* at the Theatre Royal, Haymarket, London. Dec., premiere of *Bobby Gould in Hell* at the Mitzie Newhouse Theater, Lincoln Center. *We're No Angels*, with screenplay by Mamet, released. Dec., a second collection of essays, *Some Freaks*, published.

1990   Jan., revised version of *Squirrels* included in the Philadelphia Festival Theater for New Plays season, under direction of W. H. Macy. Mar., British premiere of Mamet's adaptation of Chekhov's *Uncle Vanya* performed at the Harrogate Theatre, and at the Goodman Theatre, Chicago, in May: also recorded by BBC Television in association with WNET, New York, for transmission in 1991 (directed by Gregory Mosher; with David Warner as Vanya, Mary Elizabeth Mastrantonio as Yelena, Ian Holm as Astrov, and Rebecca Pidgeon as Sonya). Summer, his new adaptation of Chekhov's *Three Sisters* performed by Atlantic Theatre Company, Vermont. Mamet appeared on Clive James talk show on BBC Television, wrote lyrics for the Ruby Blues album *Down from Above*, released in July by Phonogram, and took part in a poker game organized by *GQ* magazine in September, writing an analysis of the session with fellow players A. Alvarez, Martin Amis, Antony Holden, and John Graham. During the year, Mamet completed the following screenplays: *Hoffa* (about the American trade union leader), *The Deer Slayer* (based on the story by James Fenimore Cooper), *High and Low* (based on the film by Kurosawa), and *Ace in the Hole*. As this book goes to press, Mamet was filming *Homicide* in Baltimore, a Cinehouse production for Bison Films, with Joe Mantegna, W. H. Macy, Natalia Nogolich, J. J. Johnston, and Colin Stinton; and a collection of poetry, *The Hero Pony*, was due for publication in the autumn.

a: Major Plays

Duck Variations

First production: St. Nicholas Th. Company, Goddard
College, Vermont, 1972 (dir. Mamet).
First New York production: St. Clement's Th., Dec. 1975 (dir.
Albert Takazauckas); trans. to Cherry Lane Th., June 1976.
First London production: Regent Th., Dec. 1977 (dir. Albert
Takazauckas).
Television: scenes in *Emerging Playwrights*, 1977 (dir. Gerald
Gutierrez); and in *New Actors for the Classics*, 1980,
including an interview with Mamet by Richard Barr (both
in TOFT Collection).
Published: with *Sexual Perversity in Chicago*, New York:
French, 1977; Grove, 1978; with *American Buffalo* and
Sexual Perversity in Chicago, London: Eyre Methuen,
1978.

---

*The scene is 'A Park on the edge of a Big City on a
Lake. An afternoon around Easter. Emil Varec and
George S. Aronovitz, two gentlemen in their sixties', sit
and talk. In fourteen 'variations', their talk covers
many subjects: some pressing, some not so urgent, but
all elaborated upon with imagination, humour (not
always conscious on the part of the speaker), and
genuine concern. And always springing from their
fascination with ducks. 'This is a very simple play',
warns Mamet in the briefest of stage directions.*

[Mamet directed the first production for his newly formed St.
Nicholas Theater Company at Goddard College, Vermont,
where he was Acting Instructor and later Writer in Residence.
He said the idea for the play came 'from listening to a lot of
old Jewish men all my life, particularly my grandfather' (*New
York Times*, 5 July 1976). In the summer of 1972 it was
performed in a double bill with *Sexual Perversity in Chicago*
in a small venue in Boston. According to W. H. Macy, a
student of Mamet's and co-founder of the St. Nicholas
Company: 'About seven people saw it.' In the autumn it

played in Chicago in the New Room of the Body Politic Theater, preceded by the monologue *Litko*. A reviewer on the *Chicago Tribune* commented: '*Duck Variations* is an intelligent, humorous verbal exercise. . . . The variations are those of attempts at love, the variations of opening and closing in which thought is jammed into the openings and frustration results. And this must always have been so for each with a variety of people. Yes, the play is close to Beckett. The theme is close to the familiar one of lack of communication.']

There is a marvellous ring of truth in the meandering, speculative talk of these old men — the comic, obsessive talk of men who spend most of their time alone, nurturing and indulging their preposterous notions. There is more here than just geriatric humour; there is also imagination and understanding, as these old parties grow impatient with each other, quarrel, make up, reveal their need for each other, and talk glorious nonsense with impassioned solemnity. They never become ridiculous or pathetic; their dignity remains intact from beginning to end. Mr. Mamet is a true and original writer, who cherishes words and, on the evidence at hand, cherishes characters even more.

Edith Oliver, *New Yorker*, 10 Nov. 1975

It is almost as pointless to describe the play's characters and set as it would be for a music critic to rave over a trombonist's dinner suit or the arrangement of the violinist's chairs. Mamet's two old men, philosophizing on the twentieth century's all-purpose theatrical park bench, spin out rhythmic exchanges like the interlocking themes of a symphony, neither sticking to the same tune for long, but passing it between themselves for extension and development until it finally returns in much the same reassuring form as it began. After a time the circling word formations become uncannily catchy, uncomfortably so; you feel there ought to be something left behind you can hum and yet all that remains is the miserable meaning of ordinary speech, the unremarkable exposure of two old men's humorously half-baked theories about natural science, half-read in *Reader's Digest*, half-understood, and time after time proved to be irreconcilable with their own commonsense and the direct observation of nature in the park. . . . Insubstantial whimsy; but written throughout with a prodigious delicacy of style.

Peter Stothard, *Plays and Players*, Feb. 1978

You can count the playwrights who haven't written about two men sitting in a park on one hand. This is just another one.

Mamet, interview for *Emerging Playwrights* programme, 1977

Sexual Perversity in Chicago

First production: by the Organic Theater Company, Leo Lerner Th.,
  Chicago, June 1974 (dir. Stuart Gordon).
First New York production: St. Clement's Th., Dec. 1975 (dir. Albert
  Takazauckas); trans. Cherry Lane Th., June 1976.
First London production: Regent Th., Dec. 1977 (dir. Albert
  Takazauckas).
Notable revivals: Apollo Th., Chicago, 16 Jan. 1979 (dir. Sheldon
  Patinkin); Nimrod Street Th., Sydney, 14 Sept. 1980 (dir. Neil
  Armfield); Weltbuhne, Berlin, Aug. 1984 (dir. Donal Berkenhoffs).
Published: with *Duck Variations*, New York: French, 1977; Grove,
  1978; with *American Buffalo* and *Duck Variations*, London: Eyre
  Methuen, 1978.

*'The action takes place around the North Side of Chicago
during a period of nine weeks one summer.' In 30 short scenes,
the play traces the brief romance of Danny Shapiro and
Deborah Soloman, whose struggle to sustain a lasting
relationship is, in the eyes of their respective friends, Bernie
Litko and Joan Webber, doomed from the word go. Bernie's
relentless recounting of wildly fantastic sexual exploits is
paralleled by Joan's bitter cynicism; his misogyny and her
neurosis infiltrate into the lives of Dan and Deb, and their initial
discovery of each other — Mamet celebrates the wonder of
mutual intimacy as well as the pain of breaking up —
degenerates into mistrust and regret. The author is wonderfully
inventive in his choice of setting for each scene: from Art
Institute to bedroom; from singles' bar to restaurant; Joan's
classroom indoctrination of her kindergarten pupils; Dan's
tentative inquiry on the nature of homosexuality while shopping
in the toy department of Marshall Fields; Bernie's outrageous
opinionating in the macho comfort of office, gym, and porno
house; culminating in the final scene, which reunites the men in
the hollow sexist triumph of the first scene, eyeing women on the
beach.*

The action and the dialogue are grounded in a specific place and time
. . . yet the truths Mamet has extracted from this common clay ring with
a simple eloquence and universality. Yes, there's plenty of frank talk,

and yes, there's a nude scene with the two lovers. But they're presented so naturally and justly that it's as if we have looked in on a part of life going by. [Stuart] Gordon, whose past work has been marked by zestful flamboyance, gives this impressionistic, intermissionless work a production that is absolutely flawless in its quiet, controlled flow. . . . Ms Custer explaining the word 'hag' to her school children, Casey silently watching the funniest *TV Reflections* you are ever going to hear, and Ms Gordon and Loeb going through the dissolution of a love affair — these scenes almost go beyond acting and into actuality. . . . This drama of human character is . . . sweet, sad, understanding, and utterly believable.

Richard Christiansen, *Chicago Daily News*, 24 June 1974

The subtly pointed incidents are so unobtrusively put together that for a while the audience is unaware that any story is being told at all — or even, perhaps, that these couples are homosexual. Also, one spends so much time laughing at the funny lines that the underlying sadness of the play comes as an aftertaste. The piece is written with grace and is very well performed in that casual, off hand 'Second City' style.'

Edith Oliver, *New Yorker*, Dec. 1975

Well. . . [it's] just, unfortunately, tales from my life. My sex life was ruined by the popular media. It took a lot of getting over. There are a lot of people in my situation. The myths around us, destroying our lives, such a great capacity to destroy our lives. Voltaire said words were invented to hide feelings. That's what the play is about, how what we say influences what we think. The words that the older [character] Bernie Litko says to Danny influence his behaviour, you know, that women are broads, that they're there to exploit. And the words that Joan says to her friend Deborah: men are problematical creatures which are necessary to have a relationship with because that's what society says, but it never really works out. It's nothing but a schlep, a misery constantly. There's a lot of vicious language in the play and that's different. The real vicious language is the insidious thing, calling somebody a little girl or this girl. That's a lot more insidious than calling someone a whore — which is also insidious, but you can deal with it. . . . [Myths] you have to go through: you have to sleep with every woman that you see, have a new car every two years — sheer utter nonsense. Men never have to deal with it, are never really forced to deal with it. . . . [They] deal with it by getting colitis, anxiety attacks, and by killing themselves. Women have babies, they have the menstrual period, for god's sake, they have children, they have something to do with the universe. . . . I kept getting hutzed by the director [Stuart Gordon at the Organic Theater] and the women in the cast, you know, 'Write parts for women'. I said, 'I don't know anything about women', they said, 'Well, you better find out, you're getting too old', so I tried. The fleshier parts are the women being candid. It's something I've been trying to do more of in the last few years. Women are very different from men, I think.

Mamet, *New York Times*, 5 July 1976

All the characters are losers. To me, it's a play about insight. . . . It's about four different ways of dealing with or failing to deal with insight. Joan intellectualizes everything, Debbie uses catchphrases, Danny jokes everything away, and Bernie tries to overpower everyone. . . . It's the way we perceive each other. If you say 'cunt' or 'cockteaser', what you say influences the way you think, the way you act, not the other way round.

Mamet, *Village Voice*, 5 July 1976

Mr. Mamet is not so interested in what brings people together as he is in what keeps them apart. . . . [He] doesn't know as much about how women are afraid of men, as he does about how men are afraid of women. Bernie is his triumph: a leisure-suited swinger (played with exquisite sleaziness by F. Murray Abraham) who regards all women with avid crudity as sexual material to be discussed, evaluated, fantasized about — from a safe distance. Mr. Mamet's stylistic virtuosity is not just a matter of snappy patterns; inside Bernie's rhetoric of lubricious appreciation, he shows us this man's terrible rage at female sexuality, that mysterious force that is so much more than he can deal with. Bernie's macho attitudinizing is a mask, made transparent for us by the playwright's art, of horrified repugnance. The point about Bernie is not, I think, that he is a 'latent homosexual' (whatever that means) but that — like Joan — he is scared, scared, scared. Bernie is not such a freak — his name is legion in every singles bar in the country — and elsewhere. Who among us is not without fear of the opposite sex, that great Other? . . . Some people have been offended by the misogyny and sexism in *Sexual Perversity* but it seems to me highly insensitive — or, in another sense, highly oversensitive — to take Bernie's fantastic crudities as the play's statement. On the contrary, this is a compassionate, rueful comedy about how difficult it is, in our fucked-up society, for men to give themselves to women, and for women to give themselves to men.

Julius Novick, *Village Voice*, 16 Aug. 1976

[Albert Takazauckas brought his production to London in 1977 — with Gina Rogers repeating for the third time the role of Joan. Ned Chaillet in

The Times of 2 Dec. 1977 noted that several newspapers had refused to advertise the play because of its provocative title, and he complained that 'the extraordinary advertising picture on the poster and programme of a woman's bare bottom and long seamed stockings . . . ensures that titillation will be the main inducement' for theatregoers. Peter Stothard, however, in *Plays and Players* for Feb. 1978, absolved the playwright of blame for 'the rows of dirty raincoats' that made up the audience for the show, and, although he felt that the play represented 'a retrogade step, a move towards the devouring standards of writing for television and film' when compared with *Duck Variations*, he praised the production. The play was revived in Chicago in 1979 at the Apollo Theater, with Jim Belushi as Bernie and Linda Kimborough, a Mamet regular, as Joan. Richard Christiansen commented in the *Chicago Tribune* on 24 Jan. that the play had now assumed 'a special and important place in the life of theatre in this city'. *Sexual Perversity in Chicago* has also been performed in West Germany, Holland, Israel, and Australia and is still a favourite with small alternative theatre companies in Britain.]

Squirrels

First production: by the St. Nicholas Th. Company, Chicago, 3 Oct. 1974 (dir. Mamet, with W. H. Macy as Arthur, Stephen Schachter as Edmond, and Linda Kimborough as the Cleaning Woman).

Notable revivals: Philadelphia Festival Th., Jan. 1990 (dir. W. H. Macy).

Published: New York: French, 1982.

My play . . . concerns two writers and the custodial staff around their office. . . . The elder writer, Arthur, feels the need for some ego-boosting and takes on a colleague. This new guy, Edmond, comes into the office with the hope of learning how to gain acceptance and notoriety in the high-pressured but diverting world of professional letters and finds his progress impeded by the fact that his mentor, Arthur, has been working on the same paragraph for 15 years. Here the plot thickens. The custodial staff of the office consists of one cleaning woman. She and Arthur were once some sort of a hot ticket, when the cleaning woman also had literary aspirations, and Arthur cut both their love affair and their artistic collaboration by plagiarizing some of her material. It's been known to happen. She is still around the building, cleaning the offices and generally being lovable, Arthur is trying to break in his new colleague, and Ed is caught in the middle trying to figure out what the heck is 'up'. I do not wish to give away the intricacies of the plot, but several things do happen.

Mamet, *Chicago Sun Times*, 6 Oct. 1974

[*Squirrels* contains some of Mamet's sharpest observations on 'the creative process' and finds some interesting echoes in *Speed-The-Plow* and *Bobby Gould in Hell*. And the story with which the two writers struggle in the first half of the piece appears to be a wonderfully sardonic variation on the themes in his earlier *Duck Variations*. According to Mamet: 'The play deals with nut-tropism, that perverse portion of the animal and human mentality which causes one to seek, to acquire gook rather than learning how to live in the moment' (*Chicago Sun Times*, 6 Oct., 1974). *Squirrels* was revised and revived under W. H. Macy's direction at the Philadelphia Festival Theater for New Plays in Jan. 1990. The Festival's artistic director Carol Rocamora explained her reasons for including Mamet's piece, which was hardly 'new', when she announced the season: 'We depart somewhat from tradition by giving the playwright an opportunity to reinvent an earlier work and make changes based on discoveries through the rehearsal process.']

Squirrels bustles with tricks from Mamet's well-known bag — nonstop rapid fire overlaps, tough verbal combat, an unerring ear for the idiomatic. Surprisingly, almost no purple language. Very funny in spots without one knowing exactly why. Playing time, one hour — seems longer — without an intermission. Not prime Mamet, despite the prime production values: players top notch, set super, incidental music cleverly conceived. Remember, this is the Mamet of fifteen years ago, warming up for his greatest hits.

Nels Nelson, *Philadelphia Daily News*, 19 Jan. 1990

American Buffalo

First production: Ruth Page Auditorium for the Goodman Th. Stage Two, Chicago, 23 Oct. 1975 (dir. Gregory Mosher; with J. J. Johnston as Donny, W. H. Macy as Bobby, and Bernard Erhard as Teach); trans. St. Nicholas Th., 21 Dec. 1975 (with Mike Nussbaum as Teach).

First New York production: Ethel Barrymore Th., 16 Feb. 1977 (dir. Ulu
  Grosbard; with Kenneth McMillan as Donny, John Savage as Bobby,
  and Robert Duvall as Teach). This production followed a showcase at
  St. Clement's Church, off-off-Broadway, Feb. 1976 (dir. Gregory
  Mosher; with J. T. Walsh as Bobby).
First London production: Cottesloe Th., National Th., 28 June 1978 (dir.
  Bill Bryden; with Dave King as Donny, Michael Feast as Bobby, and
  Jack Shepherd as Teach).
Notable revivals: Schiller-Theater, Berlin, 14 June 1980 (dir. Jorn van
  Dyck); Long Wharf Theater Company, Duke of York's Th., London,
  2 Aug. 1984 (dir. Arvin Brown; with J. J. Johnston as Donny, Bruce
  Macvittie as Bobby, and Al Pacino as Teach); Parco Th., Tokyo,
  28 May 1989 (dir. Koji Ishizaka).
Published: New York: Grove, 1976, French 1977; London: Methuen,
  1984; in *Nine Plays of the Modern Theater* (New York: Grove, 1981);
  The Obie Winners, ed. R. Wetzsteon (New York: Doubleday, 1981);
  Best American Plays, Eighth Series, 1974-1982, ed. Clive Barnes
  (New York: Crown, 1983); and condensed in *Best Plays of 1976-
  1977*, ed. Otis L. Guernsey Jr. (New York: Dodd, Mead, 1977).

*Donny Dubrow owns a junk shop on Chicago's South Side,
where he hosts the neighbourhood poker game, and where the
'action' takes place. Donny has one employee, Bobby, a young
man struggling with a drug habit, to whom he offers not only
work but companionship. Together they plan to rob a local
resident of what they believe to be his valuable coin collection
(including an American Buffalo nickel worth $90). On to the
scene strides Walter 'Teach' Cole — a poker buddy of Donny's.
He soon learns of the planned robbery, muscles in on the
operation, and, against Donny's better judgement, persuades
the store owner to oust the hapless Bobby.*

American Buffalo is classical tragedy, the protagonist of which is the
junk store owner, who is trying to teach a lesson in how to behave like
the excellent man to his young ward. And he is tempted by the devil into
betraying all his principles. Once he does that, he is incapable of even
differentiating between simple lessons of fact, and betrays himself into
allowing Teach to beat up this young fellow whom he loves. He then
undergoes recognition in reversal — realizing that all this comes out of
his vanity, that because he abdicated a moral position for one moment in
favour of some momentary gain, he has let anarchy into his life and has
come close to killing the thing he loves. And he realizes at the end of the

play that he has made a huge mistake, that rather than his young ward needing lessons in being an excellent man, it is he himself who needs those lessons. That is what *American Buffalo* is about.

> Mamet, interview in *New Theatre Quarterly*, Feb. 1988

We asked [Mamet] to direct a play [for the Goodman Stage Two], the name of which I have mercifully forgotten, and after a few days he came back . . . and said, 'Look this is a really terrible play. Why don't you do one of my plays?'. . . Then in the spring of 1975 he brought in a play called *American Buffalo*; he just came into my office and said, 'Do this play. Just do this play.' Mind you, we still barely knew each other at that point. . . . Anyway, it didn't take long to realize that this was a great, important play.

> Gregory Mosher, programme for *Lakeboat*,
> Goodman Theater, Chicago, Mar. 1982

David was living in the Hotel Lincoln in Chicago and I was working on his *The Poet and the Rent* for St. Nicholas. I went to see him one day and he says, 'I just wrote this,' and pulls out this huge script: 'It's called *American Buffalo*.' He'd just disappeared a couple of weeks and hammered this thing out. So I read it and thought, 'My God, what a play!' We did if for sixteen performances at the Goodman Stage Two; got mixed reviews, believe it or not; except for the audience and as much as people hated it, people loved it. They really were divided between: 'Big deal! Anyone can use lots of profanity', and the other people who would say: 'What are you talking about? This is the most beautiful writing that's ever come down the pipe!'

> W. H. Macy, unpublished interview with Steven Dykes, 28 Dec. 1989

The Stage Two production, superbly directed by Gregory Mosher, underlines and strengthens Mamet's theatrical vision every step of the way. Michael Merritt's setting, a Sargasso Sea of trash, and Robert Christen's shadowy lighting make visible the cluttered backwater of these lives. And the acting by J. J. Johnston as Donny, Bernard Erhard as Teach, and W. H. Macy as Bobby is so close to flawless it becomes heightened poetic reality. Mamet's mesmeric dialogue, which turns gutter language into vibrant music, is perfectly paced and unerringly delivered in Johnston's thick grunts, Erhard's whining boasts, and Macy's hesitant bleats of desperation.

> Richard Christiansen, *Chicago Daily News*, 24 Oct. 1975

Johnston as Donny has the hardest part and gives a simple well-crafted performance. The role is tough because while Teach and Bobby both go through interesting changes, Donny is the touchstone, the slow, solid personality who anchors the others and keeps them from blowing away. Whether he's being affectionate and paternal toward Bobby, bewildered by the mis-match of Teach's spiel and Teach's reality, or just playing the fall guy for one of the script's all-too-real laugh lines, Johnston's Donny is consistent and believable. . . . The lighting by Robert Christen is aptly lean, a wash of simple whites, highlighted by cold, lonely blues around the edges of the set. The set itself, by Michael Merritt, is dynamite. Here is a man who understands style and brevity. The back wall of the set is composed almost entirely of a pile of beat-up chairs, the stage is artfully and casually divided up into efficient spaces by piles of junk and a display case, and the whole thing is framed by an aurora of old chairs hung from wires. It is an exercise in tongue-in-cheek trashiness that perfectly represents the tone of the script.

Bury St. Edmund, *Chicago Reader*, 24 Oct. 1975

[This comment about the production's visual aesthetic is supported by Mamet's view of the nature and function of the setting: 'Yes, it is important in *American Buffalo* . . . that the setting is a junkshop. . . . It is a play. The audience is going to know it's a play. The important thing is — what does the junk shop mean to the play? What is the active aspect of the junk shop? Is it a place where people can support themselves, a place where they can be alone? Having made that election, then you know what kind of shop it should be' (*The Times*, 19 June 1978).]

It's Donny's play. Teach is the flashy part, you're going to get a star. But Donny's got to be able to say with a word, 'Hey, Teach, settle down'. Donny's the protagonist. It's a play about friendship and honour and the guy that goes from A to Z is Donny. And the great J. J. Johnston owned the part — in such a way that it was easy for him to give stage to other people, because he could always bring it back when it was needed.

W. H. Macy, unpublished interview with Steven Dykes, 28 Dec. 1989

If you decide, as some people have, that *American Buffalo* is really about a madman named Teach . . . you cannot do a good production of that play. [It] . . . has to be about the destruction of a relationship between two men, between a father and a son. That's the story. . . . Teach is the agent of that destruction. Then the play starts to be about American politics, about ethical choices, about capitalism, about fascism, and it has a plot. But if it is played as a psychological study of a madman, then it can't make sense; the focus of the whole thing tends to shift to the virtuosity of whoever is playing Teach and the plot and themes disappear. . . . I don't think there has ever been a production of it, that I've seen anyway, that was as good as the work J. J. Johnston and Mike Nussbaum and Bill Macy did with the play. I think Nussbaum found something in the character of Teach that nobody else has ever figured out about him — namely, that he is a poet, not a thug.

> Gregory Mosher, programme for *Lakeboat*,
> Goodman Theater, Chicago, Mar. 1982

I shiver in the theatre, listening to this dialogue — the quick alternation between the elevated and the obscene, the mixed-up syntax, the use of cadence as action, the characterization by language — and how Mamet's extraordinary ear gives us lines at once idiosyncratic and universal. . . . Mamet's extraordinary promise resides not so much in his insights into money-violence or male-female relationships, or in the tragic and comic manipulations of his understanding, as in the exhilarating perfection of the language with which he expresses it. It's a rarity in theatre to find the insights, the characterizations, the action, so deeply embedded in the dialogue itself, in its vocabulary, its idioms, its rhythms. It's a terrible burden to place upon a writer, but if Mamet can continue the astonishing advance in achievement from *Sexual Perversity* (written in 1974) to *American Buffalo* (written in 1975), I feel confident his next leap forward will give us nothing less than an American masterpiece.

> Ross Wetzston, *Plays and Players*, June 1977

I felt I was in the presence of an original voice in the American theatre, with a unique vision, intelligence, an extraordinary ear for translating real behaviour, who could capture in dialogue what is not being said, and who could do that with a class of people that is never represented in the American theatre. I couldn't believe that he was 28, and not from a lower-class background.

> Ulu Grosbard, director of Broadway production, in *Robert Duvall,*
> *Rage of a Gutter Rat* (New York: St. Martin's Press, 1985)

[But this Broadway debut (for Mamet as for *American Buffalo*) provoked some hostile reviews from the New York critics. Gordon Rogoff registered distaste for Mamet's patronizing attitude towards his trio of petty criminals; Brendan Gill called *American Buffalo* a 'curiously offensive piece of writing', not because of its language but because it offered no intellectual stimulation; and John Simon considered that the play 'marks time' through its inaction and failure to move the audience. Other views were more positive.]

The performances have great strength, and all three men are chillingly convincing. Kenneth MacMillan . . . is luminously stupid as the junkshop owner, while John Savage is equally good as the jail-bait kid who is being indoctrinated. Both actors are clever at suggesting a relationship that may be homosexual and certainly has a great deal of affection in it. The men all work well as a team, but undoubtedly the showy part is that of the third man, and this is played thrillingly by Robert Duvall. . . . Mr. Duvall's role is complex and nervy. He alternates between self-pity and wild gusts of paranoid fury. His body is like a clenched fist, his manner has the danger of a rattle snake, and he talks with a childlike tone of pure, sweet unreason.

Clive Barnes, *New York Times*, 17 Feb. 1977

The play is about the American business ethic. About how we excuse all sorts of great and small betrayals and ethical compromises called business. I felt angry about business when I wrote the play. I used to stand at the back of the theatre and watch the audience as they left. Women had a much easier time with the play. Businessmen left it muttering vehemently about its inadequacies and pointlessness. They weren't really mad because the play was pointless — no one can be forced to sit through an hour-and-a-half of meaningless dialogue — they were angry because the play was about them.

Mamet, *New York Times*, 15 Jan. 1978

[Both Bill Bryden, who directed the plays's European premiere at the Cottesloe, and actor Jack Shepherd, who played Teach, found working on the text a challenging experience.]

On first reading *American Buffalo* I recognized an absolutely distinct new voice. . . . In terms of the writing of the dialogue, the half lines, the demotic speech, one was in the presence of an absolutely unique theatre voice. I had a suspicion also that it had legs . . . it wasn't about growing up in Vermont or trouble with professors at university or rites of passage, it was about people who were not the writer. . . . I think the intellectual side of David's talent, which is incredibly subtle in the major plays, is the side that has embraced the great talents that came before him like O'Neill, Miller, Tennesse Williams . . . and these influences were a kind of classical training already finished by the time he was speaking with his own voice. . . .

It's as if there's a card game going on underneath the play — a kind of status game — who's winning? Who's on top? You play a card, that's your bid — there's a pause — the other guy doesn't tell you what his cards are and, during the pause, decides whether to outbid you or see your hand — it's a poker game. All these status games and little shifts in power, importance, and self-importance: it's ironic that we're looking at these petty incompetent thieves all struggling for power and status.

Bill Bryden, unpublished interview with Nesta Jones, 5 Jan. 1990

A lot of the Method, and the revised American version of the Method, is to do with discovering subtext, while we in *American Buffalo* found very little. . . . After three or four weeks of rehearsal we realized it wasn't written like that, people said what they meant and there was precious little subtext to it. . . . There are things floating underneath, obviously, but they don't operate in the same way that they do in a Pinter play of a similar type. . . . So after you've rehearsed it for three or four weeks, trying to play a subtext that isn't there, you're really not ready to go on in a week's time. You've realized too late that you have to play in the moment and say exactly what you mean to the person you're talking to. And that entails playing it at about ten times the speed that you would an equivalent play by Trevor Griffiths or Pinter or any good writer.

Jack Shepherd, unpublished interview with Nesta Jones, 12 Oct. 1989

Without ever once mentioning politics, Mamet has in fact written a deeply political play in which business and crime are equated and in which profit becomes an alibi for theft. What is especially good about the play, however, is that it makes its points about society through the way people actually behave. The violence at the end is shocking and yet horribly logical.

Michael Billington, *The Guardian*, 29 June 1978

It seems that the age of American jazz plays, that mountain of slapdash drug culture improvisation, is on its way out, and that writers who sweat over construction, and treat language with respect, are again finding favour. If so, that is good news; and you would have to be tone deaf to miss the music, irony, and virtuosity with which Mr. Mamet bends the Chicago idiom to his purposes in this piece. Why, then, did I find it an experience of such suffocating tedium? . . . Given Mr. Mamet's linguistic prowess, it ought to be extremely funny; and it has been admiringly compared to Harold Pinter. That strikes me as a legitimate and damning comparison. There is much in common between this play and Pinter's *The Dumb Waiter*, with the all important-difference that, where Pinter's characters are in motion, Mr. Mamet's are at a standstill. Bill Bryden's production is a decidedly sombre affair.

Irving Wardle, *The Times*, 29 June 1978

Bill Bryden's excellent production ignores the possibility of easy laughs at the expense of the characters, emphasizing the play's darker side and building slowly to the explosive climax. There are fine performances too. . . . Shepherd begins as though he is going to offer a caricature of Method acting but, after some preliminary mumblings and flailings, he offers a brilliant portrait of a paranoid neurotic, pathetically attempting to assert an individual dignity.

John Walker, *International Herald Tribune*, 2 July 1978

[Arvin Brown's production opened at New Haven's Long Wharf Theater in 1980, played successful off-Broadway engagements in 1981 and 1982, and re-opened on Broadway at the Booth Theater in 1983. Inevitably comparisons were made by the critics between Robert Duvall, who played Teach in Grosbard's 1977 production, and Al Pacino.]

Al Pacino comes into David Mamet's *American Buffalo* like a hand grenade . . . pin already pulled. . . . It is an astonishing and mesmerizing sight. . . . But if Mr. Pacino's dynamism is the first thing we notice . . . the second thing we notice is the elaborate, sometimes ostentatious, patterns of speech packed inside it. . . . Not only the words but the rhythms are odd. There is an eerily philosophical — almost maternal — sigh in both the phrasing and the reading of a line like 'knowing what you are talking about is so rare — so rare'. Mr. Pacino shakes his head sorrowingly on that second 'so rare', as though he were in mourning for the massive stupidity that is loose in the world. But it is Mr. Pacino's small-time hood who is desperately stupid, and therein, I think lies the secret of Mr. Mamet's telling use of language and of Mr. Pacino's remarkably complex and illuminating performance. When the play was done on Broadway in 1977, the Pacino role was played by that very fine actor, Robert Duvall. Mr. Duvall, however, is a straightforward, low-key, immensely plausible performer, and he tended — as I remember it — to convey genuine intelligence, certainly an intelligence superior to that of his fellows in crime. If there were pent up furies inside him that would erupt into violence before the night was done, they were valid furies: rage with the incompetence of others, rage against life's damnable odds. In which circumstances the character's linguistic pretensions served no particular purpose, unless it was to suggest that he was slightly better educated than his companions. At the time, the verbal fireworks seemed to me a too muchness: I was inclined to attribute it to the author's own verbal self-indulgence. Not here. Another thing happens here. It is the character's apparently knowledgeable vocabulary that points up his utter ineptitude. The language he uses, the rhythms he adopts, are set dead against the brutally foolish incompetence of his plans for the evening. . . . He is all language, and because he is all language, he is going to fail, which is what makes him so intensely angry.

Walter Kerr, *New York Times*, 14 June 1981

American Buffalo is so sturdy it can support radically different productions. In the 1977 Broadway staging . . . the director Ulu Grosbard saw Mr. Mamet's setting, a junk shop, as a cage emblematic of the men's tragic sociological imprisonment: When the robbery fell apart, Mr. Duvall lashed out so violently that audiences shuddered at his crazed impotence. In the 1981 Pacino version, the director Arvin Brown approached . . . from the reverse angle, seeing the junk shop as the character's only real home. His lighter treatment illuminated the absurd futility of the would-be burglars' grandiose schemes, as well as the familial fellowship that allows the men to endure their isolated, fringe existence on capitalism's scrap heap.

Frank Rich, *New York Times*, 28 Oct. 1983

There is nothing parodistic in Mamet's intentions, which aim to reveal character through language; or in his structure, which surges forward with the dense assuredness of a poem; or in his ear, which is tuned with transcriptive accuracy to the linguistic fall-out from generations of immigrant handling of the American tongue. For what I hadn't realized from the Cottesloe version is that this play is a parable about the US — not in the journalistic way of British state-of-the-nation dramas, but quietly, stealthily, with all the rich interior organization of a true work of art. . . . These three failed crooks are the waste products of the American belief in free enterprise. But while Mamet shows them as victims, it is without patronage and with respect and even love for these little people who, as he somehow makes us feel, resemble the little person in all of us. This line of thought descends from Miller, but especially from O'Neill and Tennessee Williams; there is no precedent for it in Britain; and we have failed to establish it here.

Victoria Radin, *The Observer*, 5 Aug. 1984

A lot of people thought the play was about criminals and low-lives and losers and the lumpenproletariat and I didn't think so at all. The play to me is about an essential part of American consciousness, which is the ability to suspend an ethical sense and adopt in its stead a popular accepted mythology and use that to assuage your conscience like everyone else is doing.

Mamet, *The Times*, 19 June 1978

[*American Buffalo* was Mamet's first international hit, and has been translated into Portuguese (for Brazil), Greek, Swedish, Hebrew, French, German, Dutch, Turkish, Italian, and Japanese, with major productions throughout the world. It is still frequently revived.]

Reunion

First production: 'Midnight Showcase', St. Nicholas Th. Company, Chicago, 9 Jan. 1976 (dir. Cecil O'Neal; with Linda Kimborough and Don Marston).

First major production: Yale Repertory Th., New Haven, Conn., 14 Oct. 1977 (dir. Walt Jones; with Michael Higgins and Lindsay Crouse).

First New York production: in a triple-bill with *Dark Pony* and *The Sanctity of Marriage*, Circle Repertory, 18 Oct. 1979 (dir. Mamet; with Lindsay Crouse and Michael Higgins).

First London production: in a double-bill with *Dark Pony*, King's Head Th. Club, Feb. 1981 (dir. Stuart Owen; with Don and Susannah Fellowes); trans. as 'Platform Performance', National Th., 27-28 Oct. 1983.

Television: scenes from Mamet's production in *The Playwright Directs*, WNET Camera Three, 1979 (video in TOFT Collection); ABC Arts Cable Service, 5 Feb. 1982 (dir. Monty Johnston; with Michael Higgins and Lindsay Crouse).

Radio production: with *The Sanctity of Marriage*, in *Earplay* series, 6 Dec. 1979.

Published: with *Dark Pony*, in *Two Plays*, New York: Grove, 1979; with *The Sanctity of Marriage* and *Dark Pony*, New York: French, 1982.

The play is a good minor work in a strong minor key, richly developing a threadbare situation of soap-opera familiarity. A 25-year-old woman, driven by loneliness and the probable collapse of her shaky marriage, comes to visit her 53-year-old father, an ex-alcoholic whom she has not seen in years and who now is trying to come to terms with his life. At first they chat cautiously, speaking mostly in clichés. He talks about his failed past, telling her, 'I suppose it was all for the best, but I'll be goddamned if I know how.' The daughter then pours out her own fears and tells him she wants him as a father. He in turn asks her why she is interested in a man 'you haven't seen for twenty years and who used to beat your mother.' At the play's end, recognizing each other's needs, they are hopefully trying to pick up the pieces.

Richard Christiansen. Chicago Daily News, 12 Jan. 1976

Reunion . . . is having its first full-scale production. Full-scale is a hypothetical term in the case of Mr. Mamet, for whom three characters on stage at one time is already something of a mob scene. *Reunion* has only two. . . . The play is about their relationship or, rather, it is about relationship itself. Using his characteristic clipped, oblique, and awkward dialogue — awkward in form only, because its effect is marvellously precise — Mr. Mamet has his two characters battle through all the embarrassment and misunderstanding of the reunion, and reach, finally, a kind of haven. . . . Michael Higgins and Lindsay Crouse . . . are hard and precise as two diamond chips, and diffract as many darting colours.

Richard Eder, New York Times, 22 Oct. 1977

Mr. Mamet's writing is terse but sensitive — everyday language distilled into homely poetry. . . . Words and pauses are precise. The performances are filled with specificity and certainty. Finding drama beneath the lines, Miss Crouse makes us see the desperation that is masked by confidence. Mr. Higgins enriches his character with some of the earthy, good-natured humour of an Art Carney; he is a wryly philosophical drifter.

Mel Gussow, New York Times, 19 Oct. 1979

David Mamet has written more original and striking plays than *Reunion* . . . but none I have found more touching. . . . Mamet's writing here is marked by an honest sensibility and a humanity of perception which strike home, evading all stress or pointedness. It is in this play and in this vein, as in the underestimated *Duck Variations* — sketches of solitude and groping for connection — that Mamet's most telling qualities are revealed. He is greatly aided by that admirable and always subdued actor, Michael Higgins, who really thinks on the stage; his acting bespeaks the play's theme. With lovely Lindsay Crouse, the two are a pair to whom our hearts warm.

Harold Clurman, The Nation, 1 Dec. 1979

At the first sight of them standing there, stiff as strangers, in Bernie's could-be-anyone's apartment, I was reminded of a Hopper painting. . . . Mamet, like Hopper, is a realist or a naturalist who conveys a powerful and haunting sense of the inner loneliness of modern urban life. His plays depend, however, almost entirely upon language which he uses with meticulous accuracy and the greatest economy, being blessed with a perfect ear for American speech.

Peter Jenkins, *The Spectator*, 25 Feb. 1981

It would be hard to over-praise the way Mr. Mamet suggests behind the probing, joshing family chat an extraordinary sense of pain and loss. Bernie (excellently played by Don Fellowes with a lot of winning, self-deprecatory smiles) almost seems set on wooing his daughter (the very touching Susannah Fellowes) with anti-heroic tales of his stumblebum days. The irony is that she is looking for a father, not a pal. But although the play has a strong social comment about the destructively cyclical effect of divorce ('I come from a broken home', says Carol, 'the most important institution in America'), it is neither sour nor defeatist, and shows a Rattiganesque ability to pack a lot of emotion into a single line.

Michael Billington, *The Guardian*, 25 Feb. 1981

A Life in the Theatre

First production: Goodman Th. Stage Two, Chicago, 4 Feb. 1977 (dir. Gregory Mosher; with Mike Nussbaum as Robert and Joe Mantegna as John).

First New York production: Th. de Lys, 20 Oct. 1977 (dir. Gerald Gutierrez; with Ellis Raab as Robert and Peter Evans as John).

First London production: Open Space Th., July 1979 (dir. Alan Pearlman; with Freddie Jones as Robert and Patrick Ryecart as John).

Notable revivals: Una Vita Nel Teatro, Rome, Dec. 1987 (dir. Nanni Garella; with Glauco Mauri as Robert); Th. des Mathurins, Paris, Feb. 1989 (dir. Michel Piccoli; with Jean Rochefort as Robert); Th. Royal, Haymarket, London, 31 Oct. 1989 (dir. Bill Bryden; with Denholm Elliott as Robert and Samuel West as John).

Television: in *Great Performance* series, WNET, 1979 (dir. Gerald Gutierrez, from his New York production: video in TOFT Collection).

Published: New York: French, 1977; Grove, 1978; London: Methuen, 1989; condensed version in *The Best Plays of 1977-1978*, ed. Otis L. Guernsey Jr. (New York: Dodd, Mead, 1978).

The play is a comedy. It is, in a way, an abstraction of a moment. It is not a realistic play. That is, it is not a play about two men, John and Robert, who happen to be actors, but about two actors, about two representative members of the profession, and about a turning point in the career of each. The turning point, the moment which has to be abstracted into a play, is the moment of recognition of mortality, at which moment the younger generation recognizes and accepts its responsibilities, and the older generation begins to retire. The play is divided loosely into episodes and interludes. The episodes take place while the two actors are backstage, waiting to go on, rehearsing, at the barre, and at various other spots around the theatre. In the interludes we see our actors onstage, performing, as different characters in different plays; and as the play progresses the distinction between episodes and interludes begins, slightly, to fade. . . .

Mamet, *New York Times*, 16 Oct. 1977

[Gregory Mosher, interviewed by Nesta Jones and Steven Dykes, remembers going into rehearsal 'with eighteen or nineteen major scenes pretty well finished' — then, during rehearsal, Mamet 'wrote another ten scenes, those short bridge scenes which are so much fun.' Collaboration between playwright and director resulted in the re-ordering of scenes, mostly on Mosher's suggestion, and the inclusion of a solo sequence for Robert at the end of the play, again instigated by the director. 'I kept saying there is no scene where the older actor is alone on stage. The young guy has his Henry V scene. You got to pay the old guy off.' Mosher was in favour of a 'confessional' in front of a mirror, played out front downstage, in which Robert would face the fact that he had never been a good actor; but instead Mamet wrote 'that astonishing speech at the end of the play. And I realized that it had to be staged exactly the opposite so that Robert faced upstage, facing an imaginary audience. And we got the Ghost Light on, and he had a cigarette, smoking.' Mosher realized also that he had been 'using the words to tell the story. But David said, it's not a guy talking about his story, it's a guy accepting the Tony Award, the Academy Award, and that's how they'll understand he's a failure, there he is in the lonely theatre. Well, this is the stuff of a great writer.']

The play is Mr. Mamet in a light-hearted mood. It is slight but it does not lack consequence. It has bite and it also has heart. These two incorrigible thespians win our sympathy, particularly as each, on the sly — but with the other secretly watching — tries to rehearse in an empty theatre. . . . As the cynical old poseur, Mr. Nussbaum is a Jack Gilford with a touch of John Barrymore. As the hopeful novice, Mr. Mantegna stresses the character's deliberateness. Acting is a night's work. This youth is good-natured but when his friend plays a scene in a wheelchair, he does not miss an opportunity to upstage him. Gregory Mosher's direction is nimble, giving a fluidity to the frequent shifts between reality and theatrics.

Mel Gussow, *New York Times*, 5 Feb. 1977

A Life in the Theatre is theatre to the life — a beguiling entertainment superbly acted and beautifully staged. The new comic slice of make-believe at the De Lys Theater begins and ends on a bare stage whose gloom is relieved only by the grudging beam of a work light. Between those two points, author David Mamet pays affectionate tribute to those enviable creatures who 'live to please'. . . .

What Mr. Mamet, director Gerald Gutierrez, and their cast (including Benjamin Hendrickson as a silent stage manager) have done so success-fully is to convey the feel of a strange and wondrous profession. As the senior of the two thespians, Mr. Rabb gives a performance of deft insights and subtle shadings. He is equally effective with the grand manner of the throwaway line. Even his ridiculous moments have something sublime about them. He is a joy to watch.

As John, Mr. Evans proves worthy of the partnership by showing how a talent develops and a player matures. In the most beguiling fashion, the entertainment at the De Lys demonstrates why any other way of life is unthinkable for those who have truly chosen 'a life in the theatre'.

John Beaufort, *Christian Science Monitor*, 28 Oct. 1977

I disliked *A Life*. But I soon realized that my annoyance was not induced by the fact that it was a trifle (talented artists are permitted their piffle) but by the gush with which it has been received by most of the press — celebrated as if it were the best of Mamet. . . . What we see is not a life in the theatre (not even a reasonable caricature of it) but a cliché that exists for the most part in the minds of those 'out front' who know the theatre chiefly through anecdotal hearsay. 'Ephemera, ephemera,' the veteran actor murmurs wistfully. Ephemera indeed. Very little of this has anything to do with the pain, the pleasure, the glamour, the fun or follies of theatrical life. It is all an inside joke of which the real absurdity is the sophomoric response it has produced. But that is not Mamet's fault. I look forward eagerly to his future work, but by that I do not mean further juvenilia.

Harold Clurman, *The Nation*, 12 Nov. 1977

[Alan Pearlman's British premiere production, which he set in England, was not widely reviewed, but those critics who covered it commented favourably on the play and in particular on Freddie Jones's performance as Robert, which, in the words of Colin Ludlow, writing in the Aug. 1979 issue of *Plays and Players*, captured 'the pathos of the older man with admirable control, never allowing his performance to verge into cheap sentimentality. There is great dignity not only in his portrayal of the character's pomposity and affectation, but also in the way he handles Robert's increasingly agonized awareness of his own failure and self delusion.' The Italian production was well received, Mario Sulatti in *La Republica* of 16 Apr. 1988 commenting that the quintessential Mamet dialogue managed to make the familiar theme of 'reality and fiction' fresh and entertaining. The French critics, however, felt that Michel Piccolo's production emphasized the 'playful whimsy' of the piece at the expense of its irony. Pierre Macabru, in *Le Figaro* for 3 Feb. 1989, also noted: 'Perhaps, the essence, the singularity of Mamet, his brilliance, his dynamic, is in the language, in the specificity of writing which is untranslatable into French. . . . It is possible that the nervous tension, the fluidity, the fragmented and at the same time musical character of the writing has been incompletely recreated.' The London revival of Oct. 1989 was directed by Bill Bryden, who at first considered the play 'neither flesh nor fowl'.]

It's a kind of an American play, it's a kind of English play, it's nearly like the British repertory movement. . . . The world of it seemed to me vaguer than the world of the thieves in *Buffalo* or the salesmen in *Glengarry*, but when David started to talk about it he had a real image of a Birmingham repertory theatre in his mind, which he remembered reading about in *Theatre World* and *Plays and Players*. So when I thought it might be possible, I was quite clear about saying, it must be about a fictitious Birmingham repertory theatre. There wasn't all that much to Anglicize, but I thought that was a decision that had to be taken to make it a success here. Two young producers, Bruce Hyam and Harvey Kass, came up with the brilliant idea of Denholm Elliott as Robert. During the time we rehearsed, David wrote some new scenes and I produced it on a much bigger scale than had been done off-Broadway.

Bill Bryden, unpublished interview with Nesta Jones, Jan. 1990

Mamet simultaneously satirizes the fragility of theatre and celebrates its almost masonic rituals. But what motors the play (even in an early piece like this) is the dazzling economy of the language. The first scene alone might serve as a textbook example to aspiring dramatists. On the surface, it is a nervous backstage encounter in which Robert is seeking reassurance that his performance went well: underneath it is about a lonely old actor's desire to be asked out to eat. . . . My sole reservation about Bill Bryden's production is that, by inserting an interval, it punctures the vital rhythm of the piece: surely one of Mamet's points is that a play has the same rise-and-fall curve as life itself. But there is a first-rate set by Hayden Griffin that contrasts the naked-bulb tackiness of dressing-rooms with the artificial glamour of the stage and even of the auditorium which we see in a receding perspective. Mr. Bryden also never lets us forget that, just as much as *Glengarry Glen Ross*, this is a play about work, and the competitive discipline it imposes.

It is also expertly played. . . . Denholm Elliott . . . brings out all of Robert's passion for theatre and pained insecurity. Paying tribute to 'Young people in the theatre . . . tomorrow's leaders', Mr. Elliott exudes a wrinkly testiness; he hovers around the stage-door like an elderly orphan looking for a home; and in the theatrical parodies he is diabolically funny. . . . Sam West as John proves an admirable foil. He plots precisely the character's growth from deferential nervousness to truculent independence to tuxedoed assurance; even the casual way he borrows twenty quid off the old actor in the final scene tells you everything about their reversed status.

Michael Billington, *The Guardian*, 2 Nov. 1989

[For Mamet's thoughts on the play, actors, and the institution of the theatre, see 'Regarding *A Life in the Theatre*' in *Writing in Restaurants*.]

The Water Engine

First production: St. Nicholas Th., Chicago, 11 May 1977 (dir. Steven Schachter; with W. H. Macy as Charles Lang).

First New York production: Shakespeare Festival Public Th., 5 Jan. 1978 (dir. Steven Schachter); trans. Plymouth Th. (video in TOFT Collection).

First London production: Hampstead Th., 29 Aug. 1989 (dir. Robin Lefevre).

Notable revivals: Bahen der Stadt, Kiel, 13 Dec. 1980; Dublin Stage One Th., Ireland, 4 Feb. 1981 (dir. Robert McNamara); National Th., Sarajevo, Yugoslavia, 5 Dec. 1986 (dir. David Schweizer).

Radio: in *Earplay* series, National Public Radio, Sept. 1977 (dir. John Madden). Subsequent radio productions in Germany, Austria, and Australia.

Published: New York: French, 1977; with *Mr. Happiness*, in *Two Plays*, New York: Grove, 1978.

Set in Chicago, 1934, the second year of the Century of Progress Exposition, The Water Engine *tells how inventor Charles Lang designs an eight horse-power engine which will run entirely on distilled water. The patent lawyers betray him to 'big business', which seeks to suppress the invention. When bribery fails, Lang is kidnapped, tortured, and finally killed — but his murderers are unaware that he has passed the plans on to a small boy. The narrative is punctuated by a voice speaking the words of a chain letter of the era, which claims 'all people are connected', predicts fortune or calamity depending on whether the circulation of the letter is maintained, and gives examples of the fate of those who fail to co-operate — one such having been Charles Lang.*

The Water Engine began as and still remains very much a radio drama. . . . Rather than hide the play's radio origins, [the director] flaunts them. Lines are read into microphones, sound technicians sit in a glassed-in booth to one side, and when actors are not 'on' they sit at a long table against the back wall, script in hand. Through a sly combination of John Carey's sound effects . . . and David Emmon's flexible and handsome multi-levelled set . . . the director plays *The Water Engine* as a suspenseful period-piece. . . . Here Schachter gives his audience a sight, almost a taste and a smell, of that magic time: the 'thirties in Chicago. Whether the scene is Bughouse Square, the fair's Hall of Science . . . or Lang's extraordinary lab in a garage off Halsted, Schachter and his designers create an atmosphere so rich and thick it cements the gap between realism and theatrical illusion.

Michael Vermeulen, Chicago Reader, 20 May 1977

It's the specific American myth of the suppression by monetary interests of life-giving, pain-relieving, enjoyment-provoking inventions. I mean, we've all heard these stories at one time or another: somebody once invented a light bult that will never burn out, and the company bought him out for a million dollars. Are they myths? Who knows? Voltaire said, 'There are many kinds of rumours. Some of them are true.'

Mamet, interview in
Chicago Tribune Magazine, 8 May 1977

[Steven Schachter directed the first New York production in Jan. 1978. He and designer John Lee Beatty contained the radio studio setting within a cabaret context complete with a vocal spot for Annie Hat which preceded the performance of the play.]

Where Mr. Mamet has tended to write for three or four actors at most, this has a dozen, many playing several roles. Yet it retains the author's characteristic fine control: it is another of his jewelled instruments, but it is playing stranger and more lovely music. . . . It is set on two levels of reality. First there is the Chicago radio studio of the mid 'thirties, with its announcers, technicians and performers: then there is the radio play they put on. . . . Now various kinds of slick and fairly familiar devices could be at work in all this. A pastiche of the 'thirties, for example. There is one, in fact, and it is very funny. The atmosphere of an old-fashioned radio studio, the seedy hungover look of the performers contrasted with their unctuous voices, a hilarious sound-effects man, played by Eric Loeb for the entire play like a maddened gnome. . . . Similarly the water-engine story itself is in its essentials a seamless, corny melodrama. But Mr. Mamet transforms everything. He sabotages his materials and transmutes them. By the time the play is over, apart from having been delighted, bamboozled, and confused, apart from having heard wisps of subversive counter-notions underneath each speech and movement, we end up totally seized by Lang. He becomes human innocence and struggle: defeated, but not permanently. The villains have laid hold of him, but he has mailed his blueprints to a little boy, son of the owner of his local candy store. Melodrama has become myth.

Richard Eder, New York Times, 6 Jan. 1978

[The play was revived in Chicago at the Goodman Theater in May 1985. The opening night was, according to Richard Christiansen in the *Chicago Tribune* of 7 May 1985, an occasion 'awash with sentiment'. He praised the 'richly textured revival' by Schachter, Beatty, and Jans, in which W. H. Macy re-created the part of Lang. Linda Kimborough and Colin Stinton were also in the cast, 'and, as an added touch to the reunion, the playwright himself, beaming and in a tuxedo, made a cameo appearance, presenting a bouquet of flowers to singer Annie Hat following the prolonged musical selections that preceded the staged radio drama.' Christiansen went on to say: 'This was more than a sentimental event, however. It was a complex and satisfying evening of theatre. . . . With John Lee Beatty's marvellously imagined radio studio, complete with WPA murals, combining with the shadows and highlights of Dennis Parichy's lighting to create an evocative atmosphere for this suspenseful morality tale, the Goodman auditorium was in charge of professionals who made it come alive with tension and surprise.']

Mamet is a great subverter of the pat surface message of his plays. . . . In *The Water Engine* this is achieved through the artful and very entertaining use of the play within a play. As you walk into the theatre you are confronted by the giant front panel of a 'thirties radio set, complete with illuminated wavebands. The tuner picks out several stations and then the set slides back to reveal the interior of a Chicago radio studio about to go on the air. Some of the dialogue is spoken into huge microphones that descend from the ceiling, while the rest is delivered in highly-charged discreet exchanges that teeter on the edge of melodrama. In addition there is a chorus of competing voices — soap box orators warning us off the American Dream, guides in the Chicago Hall of Science monotonously celebrating the century of scientific progress, brittle gossiping women in elevators, and a sinister, oily narrator warning about the perils of failing to pass on a chain letter. Using the form of an earnest radio play from the Depression years, director, cast, and designer collaborate brilliantly to project a bewildering world of avarice, deceit, and idealism.

Conflicts and contradictions abound. Lang's idealistic sister intones a dreamy vision of pastoral tranquillity where they will be able to retire on the profits they make for their brother's machine. Of course, in her paradise there will be no machines nor much point in having any money. Mary Maddox manages to make this character sound like a cross between the pure in heart and the lobotomized. . . . Despite this talk about Mamet's crafty ambivalence, it would be misleading to suggest that he is a playwright of ideas. The ideas are not remarkable in themselves. The great appeal of his work — for actors as well as for audiences — lies in his unerring ear for dialogue. His plays are full of theatrical opportunities. No matter how slight the scene, there is an unmistakable tension in the exchanges between the characters which brings them alive. The production makes the most of this energy.

Christopher Edwards, *The Spectator*, 9 Sept. 1989

Radio appeals to the freewheeling imagination: theatre is inevitably anchored in the concrete and visible. For all its sharp, fast, agile dialogue, *The Water Engine* offers few arresting images. It also buzzes so frantically around Chicago . . . that no scene gets a chance to build or character to develop. Radio plays can translate well to the stage . . . but they need more than a bustling, energetic plot and a single, ironic idea to sustain them. In the end, *The Water Engine* emerges as a sliver of pastiche without enough substance. . . .

Michael Billington, *The Guardian*, 31 Aug. 1989

The Water Engine is . . . an entertainment. I was born in 1947. I had no contact with old radio other than as another aspect of myth. More than myth, it's the very American idea that the real news never reaches the newspapers. Someone asked a Russian how he could live in a country with all that propaganda. He said, 'We're buffetted with propaganda. We believe none of it. You have very little propaganda. You believe all of it.' I ran into producers in New York who were thieves and I was reading a lot of Thorstein Veblen at the time — two occasions that gave rise to my writing the play. I wanted it to be about a minor mystery that all of us are confronted with, a celebration — as all good theatre should be — with the audience as communicants. The recognition of saying 'Yes, I know that. Yes, that's true.' It's not an *Oedipus Rex* or a *Death of a Salesman*, but in a minor way it's a very true play.

David Mamet, *Los Angeles Times*, 5 Feb. 1978

[See also Mamet's essays, 'Concerning *The Water Engine*' and 'Radio Drama', in *Writing in Restaurants*.]

The Woods

First production: St. Nicholas Th., Chicago, 16 Nov. 1977 (dir. Mamet; with Patti Lupone as Ruth and Peter Weller as Nick).
First New York production: Public Th., 25 Apr. 1979 (dir. Ulu Grosbard; with Christine Lahti as Ruth and Chris Sarandon as Nick: video in TOFT Collection).
Notable revivals: Stadtheater, Lucerne, 24 Oct. 1981 (dir. Jean-Paul Anderhub); New Cross Theatre, Harrogate Th. Studio, 1 Aug. 1986 (dir. Nesta Jones); Teatro Spazio Uno, 9 Dec. 1987.
Published: New York: Grove, 1979; French, 1982; with *Lakeboat* and *Edmond*, in *Three Plays*, New York: Grove, 1987.

In three scenes — 'Dusk', 'Night', and 'Morning' — the play follows a couple through initial excitement and mutual appreciation of each other and their surroundings to growing antagonism, violent disillusion, and finally an uneasy truce. Nick and Ruth escape from the pressures of the city into the clean air of the woods for a romantic weekend in Nick's family cabin. Ruth revels in the cabin's isolation, the wildlife and folklore; Nick, hesitant yet appreciative, gradually responds to her glee, joins in her stories and fantasies, and, as the lights dim on the first scene, takes her inside to make love. The weather runs parallel with the emotional current of the play, and the second scene opens with rain and the threat of storms. Ruth sits on the porch, intoxicated with the atmosphere of the blustery autumn night. Nick wakes from a dream, bad tempered and uneasy with her mood. His irritability dampens her zest and they quarrel. His attempt at reconciliation is heavyhanded and sexual; she fights him off. Her attempt is no less obvious: as a sign of her love, Ruth presents Nick with a gift — a bracelet engraved with their names. He fails to respond and the scene closes as Ruth goes in to pack. The following dawn he is contrite and hungover, but in the cold morning light their differences seem all the more irreconcilable. They argue again and violence erupts. She hits him with an oar, he retaliates, punching her off the porch. In an orgy of guilt and fear, Nick breaks down, confessing a terror of being alone in the woods and an equally terrifying need of her. She attacks him a second time, desperate to subdue his hysteria, and we are left with a final image of the exhausted couple cradling each other on the porch of the isolated cabin. He begs for comfort, and she slowly retells the story she had tried to narrate the night before — a fairy tale of children lost in a forest.

[In *Chicago Theater* for Feb. 1977, Mamet revealed the difficulties he was experiencing with the form of his new play: 'Having discarded episodic form, to write an extended action takes a lot more time. It's like making a series of sketches is so much easier than doing an oil. You take one sketch out and replace it with something else, disposable parts, but every line on the oil can change the entire picture. So learning to work with an extended form — *Buffalo* was my first play with an extended action — that takes time. And this new play, *The Woods*, is killing me.' A few days before the premiere, in an interview published in the *New York Times* on 13 Feb. 1977, Mamet discussed the play's themes. He maintained that it asks the question: 'Why don't men and women get along?', and saw the play as 'a classical tragedy' about 'the yearning to commit yourself, to become less deracinated — or more racinated'. The play was 'about change and regeneration not desolation and decay' and expressed 'a faith in human nature, perhaps'.]

The Woods shows real growth and a decidedly enlarged emotional current between the author and his work. It is less of an artifact and more an act of expression. It has Mr. Mamet's typically restricted cast — in this case a pair of lovers in a cabin in the woods — but a much wider emotional range. Sometimes, it is awkward and slow, and sometimes the deadlocks between the lovers deadlock the play. But it is moving as well as apt; it intensifies as it proceeds, and its end is hair-raising.

Richard Eder, *New York Times*, 30 Nov. 1977

Patti Lupone as Ruth is an immensely gifted actress who breathes life and beauty into every line she speaks. There is so much aching desire and warmth in her that it is almost impossible to imagine any man using her so badly. On the other hand, Peter Weller, physically well-matched with her as Nick, is almost a stick figure, a spacey automaton, so devoid of interest that it seems equally impossible for Ms Lupone to give him her lasting love, or even a second thought. . . . His role is so sketchily defined and his childish passivity so misdirected that the crucial attraction and tension between the two lovers never has a chance to develop. Other factors of the production are similarly strange. In a play, for example, where the times of day . . . are so essential to the state of emotion, why is the setting always bathed in an unchanging bright light? . . . A beautifully conceived love story, graced with some lovely passages, marred by some mundane moments, and directed by the author in a most curious fashion that throws its elegant design off balance.

Richard Christiansen, *Chicago Daily News*, 7 Nov. 1977

It lifts its back-to-the-earth zoological nostalgia from Mamet's earlier two-man *Duck Variations*, takes its hip-troubled romantic oversimplifications from *Sexual Perversity in Chicago*, and, most problematical of all, progresses almost nowhere in the reconciliation of poetic fantasy dialogue and dramatic action. . . . She wants a commitment. (Playwrights always think it's the woman.) He has less in mind. They bring their citified singles-bar mentality to rub against the intoxification of the country, leaving room for romance versus freedom, intimacy versus possession, too few of the fictions in modern coupling, plus some disconcerting redundant hogwash where pastoral clichés try passing as ageless profundities.

Linda Winer, *Chicago Tribune*, 17 Nov. 1977

Mamet's new piece has all the makings of good verse drama — it is simple, with lyrical dialogue, unpretentious, and natural. Even clichés fit into Mamet's sense of rhythm and order. . . . He just might become America's first popular verse dramatist. . . . The show seldom achieves the abstraction that I think is required for most verse dramas. At times the universal aspirations of the verse grate with the specific realism of the setting. The set, a cabin in the north woods, is simple; but sometimes not simple enough, as the ordinary presence of a chair, an oar, a door, or a bottle causes the ethereal dialogue to stumble. Mamet also insists on using no aural props — in the midst of a thunderstorm, the words are the only sound the audience hears. There is also a great deal of water in this play, either coming down in rain, or waiting for the characters in puddles — but the actors never get wet. The show is caught between two worlds: sinuous, precise, verse-prose on the one hand; and clumsy, quasi-realistic staging on the other.

John Lanahan, *Grey City Journal*, University of Chicago, 2 Dec. 1977

Miss Lahti, who gives a skilful, small-scale performance that is simply not right for this play, and Mr. Sarandon, who is monotonously petulant and uninteresting right from the start, treat the opening scene as if it were merely pre-bed chit chat. Mr. Mamet's gift is to find the speaking, prophetic force imprisoned in lame words. Miss Lahti's and Mr. Sarandon's talk is simply lame; another vignette of contemporary isolation without enough feeling in it to make us care. . . . It is a disconcerting critical experience to see a play that had looked wonderful in its first production look so poorly in its second. There is always the suspicion that the play may simply not be as good as it had seemed. At the risk of seeming stubborn in the defence of my previous opinion, I believe *The Woods* is a remarkably beautiful play. Mr. Mamet's spare, strange elusive style needs intensity and exuberance to get the best out of it. This production does not manage to supply them.

Richard Eder, *New York Times*, 26 Apr. 1979

[Mamet responded to the shortcomings of Grosbard's production, reviewed above, by re-creating his own version, with Lupone and Weller, in New York in May 1982, but again the play was poorly reviewed. Since then *The Woods* has received several productions in Europe — in England, Italy, Switzerland, and the FDR — as also in Australia and South Africa, but remains one of Mamet's lesser-known and underrated pieces. However, Mamet's continued faith in the play is evident from his following comments.]

People do not understand *The Woods* very well — I think partly because it is a play about heterosexuality, which is just not a hot theatrical topic over here. It is something that you look at in the popular media, a subject that people would rather not address — why men and women have a difficult time trying to get along with each other. . . . We don't have a great tradition of liking poetic drama. It is a play that is going to be appreciated much more in the coming years, because it's a wonderful play, a very well-written play . . . because it has a lot of meaning. It is a dreamy play, full of the symbology of dream and the symbology of myth, which are basically the same thing.

Mamet, *New Theatre Quarterly*, Feb. 1988

Lone Canoe
or The Explorer

First production: Goodman Th., Chicago, 18 May 1979 (music and lyrics by Alaric Jans; dir: Gregory Mosher; with Colin Stinton as Frederick Van Brandt.)
Unpublished.

The famous nineteenth-century English explorer, Sir John Fairfax, has spent the last five years living with the Athabascan Indians in the wilds of Canada. Believed in England to be dead, Fairfax has found peace and love among the natives and with his Indian bride, Thom, and, as the play opens, he has been hunting deer to relieve the tribe of the terrible famine that threatens it. However, his best friend and colleague from London, Frederick Van Brandt, has not given up the search for the missing Fairfax, and arrives on the scene, desperate to entice his companion back home. Van Brandt tricks the reluctant Fairfax into returning by convincing him that his reputation has been tarnished. It is in fact Van Brandt who lives in disgrace, blamed for the disastrous expedition that lost Fairfax. The two plan to leave, but their way is blocked by Thom and the tribe's shaman, Chungatte. A fight breaks out. Chungatte wounds Van Brandt. Fairfax retaliates, shooting Chungatte. The Englishmen escape, but lose their way in the Lakes. Fairfax reads Van Brandt's journal and discovers the awful truth. Van Brandt's wound proves fatal, and Fairfax is left alone with his conscience. He decides to return to the tribe and face the consequences, but receives a tender welcome from his understanding wife and forgiveness from the recuperated Chungatte. Together they will face the famine. Fairfax realizes that he is truly 'home'.

[*Lone Canoe* promised a new departure in Mamet's writing, an epic tale including six musical numbers composed by his long-time associate Alaric 'Rokko' Jans, Musical Director at the St. Nicholas Theater. Shortly before the opening, Mamet talked about the rehearsal process and the play's form and subject.]

You know how they used to raise barns in Vermont? . . . They would lay the whole structure on the ground, yoke the oxen, and, at a certain signal, pull the animals in different directions until the mortices locked together. That's how it's going with *Lone Canoe*. Nobody has any idea how the separate elements are going to fit. This is nothing like anyone of us has done before. It's all coming out of our imagination. I think it will be very special. . . . It's a completely different way for me to work. I used to start with a couple of interesting characters and find out what they're talking about. Here I roughed out the plot — a very classical structure, with each character motivated towards one thing, and each scene leading up to revelation. I'm trying to abide by Aristotle's poetical injunction, and I'm taken up with the whole notion of theatricality. . . . It's an adventure story about heroism, fame, commitment, and vanity. And it's about an English explorer, Sir John Fairfax, who gets lost in the mythological North of North America. It isn't naturalistic. Nobody talks with a British accent. It's more an England of the mind.

Mamet, *Chicago Tribune*, 25 May 1979

[The opening was destined to coincide with the annual convention of the Association of American Theater Critics which had chosen as its theme 'The Chicago Theatre Movement' — and specifically this Mamet premiere. Sixty national critics attended the first night, which turned out to be something of a debacle. However, the supportive reviewers defended Mamet's need to experiment and extend his range, eschewing the audience's expectation of 'more of the same'.]

David Mamet's *Lone Canoe* . . . is about testing, exploring, and really getting lost. And so, for the moment, is Mamet. This is a didactic myth — a serious, honest failure. . . . Chicago has had many worse evenings in the theatre, but rarely one this anguished. *Lone Canoe* . . . is Mamet's first 'play with music', yet his dialogue never has seemed less musical. . . . It is his attempt to infuse his characters with plot action, yet seldom has he been so static. One wants to suspend disbelief from here to the Empire to let him experiment and escape the tyranny of audience expectations. Still, when the feathered medicine man found yet another 'lesson to be learned from this famine', or the hero stared into space to pontificate, again, about the 'price of glory', it was hard to blame the uneasy laughter in the house. . . . This brief two-act show is Mamet's first collaboration with Gregory Mosher since the two joined forces in Mosher's new Goodman . . . and I never saw a director better able to reconcile Mamet's poetic-fantasy dialogue with dramatic action. Here, however, the two are up against a nearly unworkable combination of nineteenth-century melodrama, doctrinaire moralizing, and more simple declarative sentences than we need to get the point. Every time one starts to listen to the serious confrontation of ideas, the concentration is broken by a square English music-hall ballad or early nineteenth-century diatonic hunting tune.

Linda Winer, *Chicago Tribune*, 25 May 1979

[The play has never been revived, and the text remains unpublished. Several years later Mosher and Mamet reflected on their experiences of working on *Lone Canoe*.]

Lone Canoe was a real corner-turning for David. . . . We went counter to everything that was expected: there were no 'dirty' words, the music and lyrics had a nineteenth-century feel, it wasn't a comedy, there was no cynicism anywhere. And people said, 'This is the guy who wrote *Sexual Perversity in Chicago*? What is this, a joke?' To put it mildly, most people didn't like it very much. But I've never regretted it (although I would direct it differently now) for one moment.

Gregory Mosher, programme for *Lakeboat*,
Goodman Theater, Chicago, Mar. 1982

I have lots of unfinished plays that were never produced because they didn't work, but since *Lone Canoe* did get produced, I feel I owe it something. A lot of my rage at the time was directed against myself, and, finally, I think I may have just been too damn earnest about it.

Mamet, *Chicago Tribune*, 26 Feb. 1982

Lakeboat

First production: by Court Th., a project of the Milwaukee Repertory Th., Milwaukee, 24 Apr. 1980 (dir. John Dillon; with Larry Shue as Joe).

Notable revivals: Stage Two, Long Wharf Th., New Haven, 2 Feb. 1982 (dir. John Dillon; with Larry Shue as Joe); Goodman Th., Chicago, 2 Mar. 1982 (dir. Gregory Mosher; with Mike Nussbaum as Joe).

Published: New York: Grove, 1981; French, 1983; with *The Woods* and *Edmond*, New York: Grove, 1987.

There are eight men on 'Lakeboat', two officers, five veteran seamen, and a college boy making his rite of passage on a summer job. Their ship, carrying steel on the Great Lakes, is a small limbo planet of its own, divorced from the land and out there in the middle of nowhere. The men, like so many of Mamet's characters, are wanderers and vagrants without families, boasting of cars and guns and action and sex and sighing over lost opportunities, wasted lives, and growing fears. The hours pass, the ship moves ahead, the shifts change, and, through it all, amid the overheard conversations, reflective monologues, and heated exchanges, there is talk of a fellow crew member whose fate on shore is a subject of concern and speculation. Alone and fearful and bored, the men come together in search of warmth and comfort, absurd and silly creatures of sensitivity and dignity. Their talk is ridiculous, hyperbolic, touching, fantastic. . . .

Richard Christiansen, *Chicago Tribune*, 5 Mar. 1982

[In the Grove Press editions of the play, Mamet writes: '*Lakeboat* was first staged by the Theatre Workshop at Marlboro College, Marlboro, Vermont, in 1970. It then sat in my trunk until John Dillon, Artistic Director of the Milwaukee Rep, discovered it in 1979. John worked with me on the script, paring, arranging, and buttressing; and its present form is, in large part, thanks to him.' Later, in 1987, Mamet described the production as 'wonderful, beautiful, unforgettable'.]

Our dramaturg had known David in Chicago and David had given him the play and he brought it to me. . . . My first meeting with David — I was very apprehensive because I had red marks all over my script, places where I felt there should be cuts, places that needed to be clarified. But I discovered that we both had been doing the same thing, which was going through the script and cutting. Then there followed a lot of meetings in various locations. . . . I would describe what I felt was a dramaturgical problem and he would work it out on the typewriter, and come up with something completely different. I felt it was very important that the audience got the throughline. . . . We then had an in-house reading and David and I continued to work on it. . . . I met with him in Hollywood while he was working on *Postman*, and we were in a restaurant and there was this well-known Hollywood character actor, used to play a lot of tough guys. David pointed and said, 'Joe Litko'. Well, that threw me, because it wasn't at all how I'd seen him. So when David came to see the show I was worried because Larry was a much softer version, but David was enraptured. . . . It was really a magical time. . . . We tried to keep the design simple, a few sound cues to create atmosphere. Simple. The play is chamber music.

John Dillon, unpublished interview with
Nesta Jones and Steven Dykes, Milwaukee, Nov. 1989

Mamet worked the lake while a college student, and Rep's John Dillon comes from a seafaring family. The result is a vivid portraiture of the crusty seamen who somehow manage to string together entire sentences of four letter words. The 80-minute play comes close to being two plays. In the first, Mamet displays his ear for the humour and absurdity of everyday speech. His characters talk in circles while using conversational patterns familiar to everyone. . . . Conversations are genuine and funny, and they repeatedly show the inadequacies of men's rough language. About halfway through the play, Mamet seems to shift gears. The humour is left behind, and we get a serious look at Joe, a weary veteran seaman who struggles with the difficulty of expressing his frustrations and broken dreams. Joe is haltingly eloquent about his youthful hope of becoming a dancer, the functional beauty of a bridge, his self-destructive impulses. . . . Larry Shue gives a beautiful performance as Joe. Understated and poker-faced, he shuffles about Laura Maurer's clever set like a man who has grown old before his time.

Damien Jaques, *Milwaukee Journal*, 2 May 1980

Lakeboat is Mr. Mamet's *Life on the Mississippi* — the artist as a young river pilot, or in Mr. Mamet's case, lakeboat steward. Through his eyes, we see a cross-section of flavourful characters, imparting lore, both land-locked and seaworthy. . . . The work is close in spirit to the author's other early short plays, combining the counterpoint style of *Sexual Perversity in Chicago* with the shaggy taletelling of *Duck Variations*. Whatever the provenance of *Lakeboat*, the writing is effortless and intuitive. . . . Mr. Mamet's crew repeatedly reveal sudden turns of personality, delivered with such sincerity that we come to be believers — and some of the tales are as tall as Twain.

Mel Gussow, *New York Times*, 17 Feb. 1982

It would be nice, I think, to come to *Lakeboat* without any expectations and absolutely fresh and unprepared for this experience. . . . Yet here it is in its Chicago premiere on the main stage of the Goodman Theater, with Mamet now a celebrated playwright, and in front of a divided opening-night audience, half the house too eager to appreciate, the other half uncomfortable or angered by its occasionally vulgar language. Mamet's plays do that to an audience's expectations because he doesn't construct a plot or create depth in the way we're used to having them presented to us. His plays are intricately layered and woven, but they come at us tangentially in short, sometimes overlapping scenes; with no great concern for direct story lines. Their characters often repeat and re-repeat the crudest of gutter words, yet the sound and sense of those words can be intensely lyric.

Richard Christiansen, *Chicago Tribune*, 5 Mar. 1982

The play examines the idea of dreams — dreams of yourself. When Joe says, 'I wanted to be a dancer'. . . it's just like that famous line that Brando has in *On the Waterfront* in the back of the cab: 'I coulda been a contender.' These men talk about all the things they could have done but didn't; yet the play is never pathetic, it's never saying, 'Oh God, let's feel sorry for these guys.' They are simply themselves. David manages to convey the story of these men without an ounce of contempt or condescension, but at the same time he captures the elements of lunacy in their world. He has been able to present them in all their dignity, yet show their shortcomings in the most powerful and hilarious kind of way. You start with the whole idea that life is made up of choices, that man's fate must be balanced by a very active use of the will. I think that isolation is the central theme of the play. But at the same time *Lakeboat* is about the sense of community that these people have about them, which is what balances the isolation and gives both images their meaning. . . . Each character has some fantasy that he's thinking about here, in the midst of this isolated boat, that world in the middle of the 'inland seas'. Each of the actors will have to construct that individual's fantasy; my job is to see that those fantasies are in harmony with the other fantasies within that community, as well as consistent with the little bit of text which David provides.

Gregory Mosher, programme for *Lakeboat*,
Goodman Theater, Chicago, Mar. 1982

Edmond

First production: Goodman Th., Chicago, 4 June 1982 (dir. Gregory Mosher; with Colin Stinton and Linda Kimborough).

First New York production: Provincetown Playhouse, 27 Oct. 1982
    trans. of Goodman Th. production (video in TOFT Collection).
First British production: Tyne-Wear Company and English Stage
    Company, Newcastle Playhouse, 7 Nov. 1985 (dir. Richard Eyre;
    with Colin Stinton as Edmond, Miranda Richardson as
    Glenna, Connie Booth as Edmond's wife, and George Harris as
    the Preacher/Prisoner); trans. to Royal Court Th., London, 3 Dec.
    1985.
Notable revivals: Staatstheater, Stuttgart, 4 Oct. 1986 (dir. Gerd
    Bockmann).
Published: New York: French; Grove, 1983; London: Methuen, 1986
    (Royal Court Writer Series); with *Lakeboat* and *The Woods*, New
    York: Grove, 1987.

---

*Edmond Burke is a successful business man of 34 who lives with
his wife in Manhattan, New York City. He visits a fortune-teller
who convinces him that he is a special person living in the
wrong place and that his world is falling apart. He promptly
leaves his wife and plunges into the nightmare underworld of
the city, peopled by whores, pimps, and three-card-trick players.
Edmond is mugged and robbed, buys a knife at a pawn shop,
kills a pimp, sleeps with a waitress who professes to be an
actress, and in a fit of madness murders her. He is finally
arrested, convicted, and imprisoned. Once in prison, he severs
his relationship with his wife, refuses to see visitors, undergoes
a virtual breakdown when sodomized by his black cellmate, and
gradually comes to terms with his fall from grace, conclud-
ing that behind every fear hides a wish. The play closes with
Edmond and his cellmate casually philosophizing at the end of
the day. Their conversation over, Edmond kisses him goodnight.*

Edmond is a morality play about modern society. Jung said that sometimes it really is not the individual who is sick, but the society that is
sick. I don't know whether I believe that completely or not, but that is
what *Edmond* is about — a man trying to discover himself and what he
views as a sick society.

Mamet, *New Theatre Quarterly*, Feb. 1988

[Mamet, according to Gregory Mosher in interview with Nesta Jones
and Steven Dykes, always refers to *Edmond* as his 'love-letter to New

York'. Mosher considers *Edmond* to be a 'very dark' play. 'Except, I think you've got to work on it as a play about redemption. And you have got to make that kiss inevitable. It's certainly the most controversial of the plays. About a third of the audience didn't leave at the end of the show. The session would move to the bar and they'd talk about the play, particularly the racial aspects of the play.']

Edmond is the portrait of a man swept away by a wave of events beyond his control, as bleak and relentless as that in Büchner's *Woyzeck* — a play with which it shares common ground. The title character of Mr. Mamet's drama . . . swirls from rejection to desperation to a homicide that seems almost involuntary. Woyzeck is the essential uneducated common man; Edmond is a middle-class contemporary suburbanite, but Mr. Mamet clearly sees him as a representative of an abused underclass. . . . The writing is terse, the scenes staccato; by comparison, Mr. Mamet's other work seems verbose. The play is short and intermissionless. Mr. Mamet has squeezed it almost dry of humour and colour, and what little comedy remains seems accidental. At times the work seems like a skeleton for a play still to be fleshed.

Mel Gussow, *New York Times*, 17 June 1982

When the drama stops briefly to allow Mamet, the philosopher, to contemplate man's destiny, it is in danger of becoming studied and pretentious in its dialogue. But when Mamet concentrates on the singular rage and futility of Edmond lashing out for some human feeling, the drama is a searing, stunning work of theatre . . . a play of shattering yet exhilarating ferocity. Its savagery, which summons up the demons in all of us, is cleansing. And, for all its brutality, it is ultimately a most humane and compassionate work.

The play is illuminated on every side by a production of beautiful simplicity, masterfully paced and modulated. Gregory Mosher, directing his fourth Mamet premiere, has staged the drama with piercing clarity, so that nothing stands in the way of the intense action and spare dialogue. No gesture is wasted, and in a drama where one wrong note could shatter the agony or push the play into parody, every moment is played perfectly.

In the clean black box that has been made of the Studio's stage, Kevin Rigdon's evocative, precisely timed lighting and Bill Bartelt's basic scenery (a table, a few chairs, and a bed) shift from one chamber of city horrors to the next with cinematic fluidity. Even an exit door leading off from the stage is ingeniously used to striking effect. As Edmond, Colin Stinton . . . is in amazing control of his furies. He is a shade too young for the part, but his passage from buttoned-down businessman to wounded, raging animal is sustained without a flaw, and his final scenes, when he has come through the fire to an awesome serenity, are staggering in their hushed power.

Richard Christiansen, *Chicago Tribune*, 7 June 1982

[Mamet was interviewed in the *New York Times* of 24 Oct. 1982, a week before the transfer of the Goodman production. 'The city's nuts', he claimed. 'It's a society that's lost it's flywheel, and it's spinning itself apart. That's my vision of New York. It's a kind of hell.' He went on to describe the play as 'a fairy tale, a myth about modern life. . . . It's a play about an unintegrated personality. . . . Throughout the play, people are divided by sex, by sexual preference, by monetary position, by race. . . . [Edmond] thinks he's free, that he's faced the truth of himself. Only at the end of the play, after having completely destroyed his personality, does he realize how incredibly destructive and hateful an attitude that is. In fact, he winds up in a homosexual alliance with a black guy. Because of that alliance, because he resolves those basic dichotomies, I think it's a very, very hopeful play.' Mamet agreed that his play 'has something to do with *Woyzeck*', but said that a more influential source was Theodore Dreiser's *An American Tragedy*: 'I've read that book ten times since I was a little kid . . . and it's always struck me what a great achievement it would be if I could one day write a scene to make people understand why somebody killed.' He emphasized again, however, that 'there are moments of real beauty in the play, and I think that rather than it being about violence, it's a play about someone searching for the truth, for God, for release.' The New York critics were, however, less than kind, with a few exceptions — such as Jack Kroll, who described *Edmond* in *Newsweek* on 8 Nov. 1982 as 'a riveting theatrical experience that illuminates the heart of darkness'. Mamet's response to the hostility of the New York reviewers and audience was, ultimately, philosophical.]

It's talking about a lot of things that really get under the skin. When people have suspended their conscious process of ratiocination by indulging in a theatrical thing, and you start talking about racial guilt, homosexual panic, impecuniosity, and misogyny in a way that's fairly clear, it's naturally going to upset a lot of people who are anxious about those things. And that happened.

Mamet, *Chicago Tribune Calendar*, 17 June 1984

In the programme there was talk of an American Woyzeck. Gerd Boeckmann extended the similarity of characters considerably. Edmond was a Candide, a Peer Gynt, an Everyman. . . . In an environment of alleged adventure Edmond seeks to be free of an unhappy marriage and enervating emptiness (Peer Gynt?). . . . The world is nothing but a piece of shit and you can only exist in the world in order to hate and to oppress so that you don't get oppressed yourself (Candide?). . . . Last stop after a fatal stab with the knife (Woyzeck) is prison and it is there that Edmond recognizes true freedom that is not dependent on surface reality; he understands everything as a fate allotted to him and he respects the bond of guilt and penance (Everyman or even Raskolnikov). As long as David Mamet describes situations, rips through dialogue, outlines characters, it is fun to watch and to listen. But beware when this magnificent consumer-dramatist starts to philosophize! His beautiful staccato drama is then immediately finished with and dullness takes its place.

Heinrich Domes, *Suedwest Presse*, 6 Oct. 1984

It was like laying this huge American turd in the middle of an English garden. I think that's the way I described it, after we'd performed the British premiere of . . . *Edmond* for an audience in Newcastle. I may have been more specific and said a 'New York turd', for the play is Mamet's harsh vision of a man's life falling apart amidst the crime and the violence of that city. . . . I had performed the dark, violent Edmond in both Chicago and New York, where audiences were prepared by their own experiences to roll with the punches, and even laugh with recognition at its verbal, physical, and spiritual obscenities; but in a small city in Northern England, I suddenly felt embarrassed. From that audience, according to director Richard Eyre, there was 'nothing but the sound of gobs being smacked', and I had only been in England long enough to imagine genteel English ladies and gentlemen, with reddened faces, discreetly making for the door. I needn't have worried. After living for a decade each in both Chicago and New York, I had to go to Newcastle to get robbed for the first time, and to see someone accosted in the subway — in much the same way as depicted by a scene in the play. Whether they knew it or not, the people of Newcastle were just as ready for *Edmond* as those in other urban environments. Indeed, we may have been bringing them the proverbial coals. Later, at London's Royal Court Theatre . . . audiences had no problem relating to the harsh realities it depicted, even though set in New York.

Colin Stinton, *The Guardian*, 24 Jan. 1989

The picaresque fable is staged with wonderful fluency by Richard Eyre, William Dudley's emblematic settings . . . materializing within a black box topped off with minimal steel girders and catwalks which produce one magical moment when the hat lady makes a descending entrance.

Colin Stinton has come from Chicago to repeat his performance as Edmond and combines a curious emotional blankness with a pernickety sense of decency in every flagrantly indecent situation. There is here a remarkable sense of a character wanting to break free and going about doing so with rare indelicacy and inefficiency. Edmond is transformed into a tragic victim. . . .

In *American Buffalo* and *Glengarry Glen Ross*, Mamet composed complex stage poems rooted in particular speech rhythms and argots. In *Edmond* he reverts to the revue shutter style of earlier plays like *Sexual Perversity in Chicago* and *Duck Variations* while simultaneously moving into new structural and tragic dimensions.

Michael Coveney, *Financial Times*, 4 Dec. 1985

It was through playing Edmond that I really realized what was meant by catharsis. . . . People would say 'what a difficult journey you have to make during that play, such a long demanding part'. In fact it's not that long, about ninety minutes — but he goes through so much. Actually, it was always quite energizing to do it. Once you start you get so caught up in it, and also because the casts were so good in both productions, all I had to do was show up and they would do *Edmond* to me. You get caught up as the character is caught up, it could happen to you. The character himself would take the downfall — the fact of it happening would get the adrenalin going. I used to leave feeling terrific because in a way it purged all those feelings of guilt, fear, terror of violence or whatever, that we harbour and I could come out feeling refreshed by it. I always enjoyed doing it. I can recommend it as therapy

Colin Stinton, unpublished interview
with Nesta Jones and Steven Dykes, July 1989

Glengarry Glen Ross

First production: Cottesloe Th., National Th., London, 21 Sept. 1983 (dir. Bill Bryden).

First American production: Goodman Th. Studio, Chicago, 6 Feb. 1984 (dir. Gregory Mosher).

First New York production: John Golden Th., 25 Mar. 1984, trans. of the Chicago production (video in TOFT Collection).

Notable revivals: Habimah National Th., Tel Aviv, 7 Aug. 1984 (dir. and des. Daniel Freudenberger); Alexander Th., Johannesburg, 11 Apr. 1985 (dir. Bobby Heaney; des. Andrew Botha); Abbey Th. at the Peacock, Dublin, 8 May 1985 (dir. Louis Lentin; des. Frank Halliman Flood); Th. National de Marseille, 19 Nov. 1985 (dir.

Marcel Marechal; des. Michael Merritt); Teatro Stabile, Genoa,
16 Jan 1986 (dir. Luca Barbareschi); Sydney Opera House Playhouse,
10 Apr. 1986 (dir. Neil Armfield); Th. de Vidy, Lausanne, 2 Dec.
1986 (dir. Jean-Pierre Malo); Teatterikor Keakoulu, Helsinki, 9 Feb.
1989 (dir. Antti Einari Halonen); Haiyuza Th., Tokyo, 8 Feb. 1990
(dir. Toru Emori; des. Setsu Asakura).

Published: New York: French, 1983; Grove, 1984; London: Methuen,
1984.

---

*Four real-estate salesmen — Shelly Levene, Dave Moss, George
Aaranow, and Richard Roma — are competing in a sales
contest which is nearing completion. The one who sells the most
lucrative plots becomes the top man on the board (sales graph)
and wins a Cadillac, the second a set of steak knives, and the
remaining two get fired. To achieve a sale the men first need
leads (appointments) preferably with a gullible prospect (client)
who can be persuaded to sign a cheque to close the deal. This
life and death struggle with its inflexible 'Catch 22' rules (only
salesmen who successfully close contracts are given leads) is
initiated by the unseen bosses of the real-estate outfit, Mitch and
Murray, whose shady operation is run from a downtown office
by a lackey manager, John Williamson. Act One comprises three
conversations in a Chinese restaurant. The first is between
Levene and Williamson. Levene, formerly a top-seller, is down
on his luck: his commissions for the month are low and his
prospects of winning the Cadillac are remote. It soon becomes
apparent that the desperate Levene is selling himself to obtain
the precious leads from Williamson, whose power rests in his
control over their distribution. In the second conversation, Moss
is outlining a plan to Aaranow to break into the office to steal
the leads and sell them to a rival firm. Moss tries to enlist
Aaranow as a partner, accusing him of being an accessory to
the crime simply because he listened. Despite Moss's abrasive
manner, the encounter has all the signs of an anxious sell. The
final conversation centres on Roma's insidious sales approach
to persuade James Lingk of the not-to-be-missed opportunity to
own a plot of undeveloped land in Florida — Glengarry
Highlands. In Act Two the salesmen arrive next day at the office
to find it ransacked and the leads missing. Baylen, the police
officer in charge of the investigation, interviews them all in turn.*

*The 'whodunnit' develops alongside a continuing interaction
between the salesmen which eventually focuses on Levene and
Roma, revealing both their mutual regard and the identity of
Moss's accomplice.*

[Harold Pinter, to whom the play is dedicated, was instrumental in
getting the National Theatre of Great Britain, of which he was an
Associate Director, to stage the world premiere of *Glengarry Glen
Ross*. Bill Bryden, director of the Cottesloe company, which had
previously staged the European premiere of *American Buffalo*, was
equally impressed by the play: 'I thought, this is an absolute masterpiece, this is it, this is the best American play for years.' Peter Hall,
Artistic Director of the National Theatre, was of a like mind, and the
play went into production in the summer of 1987, with Mamet in
attendance at rehearsal. Bryden commented: 'There must have been
moments when he thought, "Why am I explaining to this guy from
Purley what it's like to be a salesman in Chicago?" and so on.' But
Mamet was used to a process in which writing is 'never divorced from
production.' In the event very little of the text was changed: according
to Bryden, 'We cut about one line and added about four words.' The
director's approach to rehearsing the play was entirely through the text:
'We didn't do any improvisations, but there were discussions about the
off-stage characters. We had a real sense of the Nyborgs — and we
made up bits of the play that don't happen on stage. We worked through
the text trying to discover the people's energy — out of their energy
came their desperation. David did tell us about some of the guys he
worked with in the salesmen's office — the desperation in the play is
somewhat less than it really was.' Mamet confirmed this in an interview
in *The Guardian* on 16 Sept. 1983, before the opening: 'I wanted to
write a play about my time in a real-estate office — it was much wilder
than in the play — and that's what it's about . . . people who live by
their wits and didn't have a college education. What they've found is a
profession which allows people without education but a lot of native
intelligence the possibility of making a lot of money.' He went on to
say: 'It's a very good American value which our liberal bourgeois
culture has rather eschewed: to look at things for what they are, to
decide what you want and to act accordingly. Living in the age of the
welfare state, in the age of liberal expectations, of hypocrisy, that idea
has to a large extent vanished. I'm not talking about social pragmatism
but about individual pragmatism. The way to survive as an individual is
not to look for an answer from abstracted ideals but rather to look
around you as an individual to see what it is you want as an individual
and what will get it for you. It's the good part of the Frontier philo-

sophy — the part nobody ever subscribes to. The part that everybody subscribes to is, let's go out and take everything we want and kill people to get something for nothing. I'm not defending it or attacking it, I'm discussing it. We have a tradition of free speech in America that everyone can say whatever they want as long as everyone agrees with it.' Bryden recognized 'how much of a risk David was taking to have the world premiere of an important American play not in America. We realized the importance of the moment. We knew all the American critics would come to London to see their own play and there was a lot of pressure on us, but it was all very exciting when it paid off.' Bryden had always known that 'it would take a bit of time for the audience to have the dictionary of the play but we also knew never to be slow, never to try to explain it to an audience, just do it.' The play and production received almost universal praise from the critics and played to full houses throughout its run.]

I wouldn't class the play with *Death of a Salesman*, which poignantly shows how the American dream of individual initiative has been soiled by the corrupt ethos of the sales-pitch. But what Mamet does is show how the fight for survival bends personal morality: in this world you implicate a colleague in crime for the sake of a puny reward and you proclaim fellow-feeling while grabbing someone else's territory. Mamet stops short of attacking the system; but he paints a vivid, cruel, often hilarious portrait of a hermetic and tacky order in which people camouflage fear under a wealth of blue-streaked street-talk.

Bill Bryden's production, with the help of two very good sets by Hayden Griffen, exactly catches this feeling of a nervous, closed society. And there are riveting performances from Jack Shepherd as the white-suited hustler backing away from people as he gets more vocally aggressive; from Derek Newark as a flannel-suited blusterer bullying the very man from whom he most needs help; and from Karl Johnson as the sweaty-palmed office-manager surveying his desperate charges with the quiet guilt of one who never has to venture out into the jungle of the hard sell.

Michael Billington, *The Guardian*, Sept. 1983

In the last scene of the first act we are shown the sales end of the operation, in the form of a chance meeting between Jack Shepherd and Tony Haygarth. It is in the delineation of the relationship between rep and client that Mr. Mamet's writing really excels, as Mr. Shepherd manoeuvres his victim into the position of maximum vulnerability. The trick, in this case, is to make the client grateful for the attention of the salesman. You feel that no one has ever talked this way to Mr. Haygarth before. No one has ever shown such a willingness to spend a dull evening in a deserted Chinese restaurant amusing him, impressing him, making him feel good. And as it turns out in the second half, when Mr. Haygarth has come to the office, on his wife's orders, to cancel the deal that has been struck, it is the client who feels that he is letting the salesman down. Whatever evidence there might be to the contrary, Mr. Haygarth torments himself with the idea that he is losing, in Mr. Shepherd, the best friend he ever had. . . .

James Fenton, *Sunday Times*, 25 Sept. 1983

[In the first American production, at the Goodman, the majority of the cast were already familiar with Mamet's work, and had either lived or worked in Chicago where the play is set. An ensemble feeling developed informally through living, eating, drinking in the same hotel, and participating in background 'research', which involved visits to the Northwest Side neighbourhood where Mamet envisioned the real-estate office and the Chinese restaurant that inspired the setting for the first act. The director, Gregory Mosher, also created a series of improvisations which encouraged antipathy between the salesmen and Williamson, dramatized the setting up of the sales contest, and so on. Herb Cohen, the author of *You Can Negotiate Anything*, spoke to the actors; and salesmen from International Business Machines and Xerox, and a Fuller Brush saleswoman (Mamet's favourite), lectured to them on sales technique.]

Mamet seems to get more original as his career develops. His antiphonal exchanges, which dwindle to single words or even fragments of words and then explode into a crossfire of scatological buckshot, make him the Aristophanes of the inarticulate. He makes the filthiest male-to-male dialogue pop with the comic timing of Jack Benny or pile up into a profane poetry that becomes the music of desperation. In *Glengarry Glen Ross* Mamet appears to be trying to wed the uncompromising vision of moral primitivism in *American Buffalo* with a more accessible, even commercial appeal. The move is a good one, but it costs him something. His second act introduces elements of relatively conventional plotting and farce that occasionally wobble; the resolution of the real-estate-office rip-off doesn't quite ring true.

Jack Kroll, *Newsweek*, 9 Apr. 1984

[The] salesmen . . . for all their ruthlessness and competitiveness, have . . . managed to assume a kind of unexpected camaraderie, largely in opposition to such 'fucking white bread' as Williamson. Except for him,

Roma tells us, 'everyone in this office lives on his wits'. But the race is becoming extinct. 'It's not a world of men,' reflects Shelly, 'it's a world of bureaucrats, clock watchers, office holders — we're a dying breed.' Dying they may be, but for Mamet this sleazy, smarmy race of losers still have a volatile energy, even an elegiac aura of heroism. The powerful tensions he has uncovered between the ethnic underclass and the WASP functionaries who administer its employment opportunities pick the scabs off a lot of ancient half-healed wounds. Gregory Mosher, has capitalized on his association with Mamet to create a forward momentum that is relentless while deepening each of the performances. Robert Prosky as Levene maintains a manly resolve and courage in the midst of squeezed grey defeat; Joe Mantegna's Roma, with his patent leather hair, gold cuff links, and pinkie ring, essentializes the splendid vulgarity of a merchant of manipulation; James Tolkan is wired and taut as Moss; Mike Nussbaum plays Aaronow like a foreign beagle, his sad eyelids drooping over his perpetually woeful countenance; and J. T. Walsh is steely cold as the meticulous Williamson, whose only physical defect is a spreading bureaucratic bottom. Michael Merritt's sets are brilliantly rendered disaster areas, especially the cinder block office, and Nan Cibula's costumes provide an authentic polyester look for men who have a weakness for terrible clothes.

Like *American Buffalo*, *Glengarry Glen Ross* is to my mind a genuine Mamet masterpiece, a play so precise in its realism that it transcends itself and takes on reverberant ethical meanings. It is biting, pungent, harrowing, and funny, showing life stripped of all idealistic pretences and liberal pieties — a jungle populated with beasts of prey who nevertheless possess the single redeeming quality of friendship. It is a play that returns tragic joy to the theatre — the kind of understanding O'Neill gave us in his last plays, facing painful truths with courage and thereby leavening profound pessimism with profound exhilaration. It is a play that shares the secret implicit in all fine works of dramatic art — that such truths are much more potent shown than told.

Robert Brustein, New Republic,
reprinted in Who Needs Theatre, 1987

All that you need in David's play is what's necessary to tell the story. The point about the Chinese restaurant is not that they're eating, but that that's their real office. That's their clubhouse, that's where they hang out, that's where they make phone-calls, that's where they meet clients . . . it's their place of business. Not the office! The office is the storeroom for them, as much as it is anything else. So it's a red herring to have them eating. . . . The actors were desperate for food, of course, because actors love props, it helps them relax. Jimmy Tolkan begged me for chop-sticks, begged me for them. I said, 'You can have them left over, and if you start playing with them you have to give them up.' So that was that. So all the attention became on the action of the first scene. The props became money. So in the first scene with Williamson and Levene you get 800 pairs of eyes focusing on a $10 bill. That's great fun, but it's almost impossible to do if the stage is littered with Peking Duck and cold brown rice. The modulation, staging-wise, just became: are they leaning into each other, are they leaning out? So it meant a lot when Jimmy Tolkan was sitting in his bunkette with the curve at the end, and he's got his leg up on the bunkette, and all of a sudden it was his office — because nobody was gonna come and tell him to put his leg down. That's the only reason they ever came to this restaurant. The original idea at the theatre was to have a bare stage with lots of tables and it was very beautiful, a lovely restaurant with pools of light picking out the tables, but it had nothing to do with the play. The thing was that this was not a public space but a private space.

The show got up, it looked fine, the audience enjoyed it, it was screamingly funny, the first act played like *Dambusters*, the second act was playing great — *but* David was not happy with it. It was clear that something was missing in the production, but I didn't know what it was. And the audience was vastly approving of it every night, so it wasn't like we were hitting the Dead Spot which would obviously need to be fixed. And he wrote me a letter, finally. He said, 'Look, this play is not like *American Buffalo* — it is not fuelled by love. These are guys who kick the other person when he is down, and you must find this in the production.' Well, then to me it was easy. I understood what the problem had been. There was still an air of decency about these fellas. You know, they were wily, they were funny, they were conniving, selfish, and greedy, but they weren't vicious. The sheer pleasure of Shelley telling off Williamson had been sort of business-like — a man saying what he was absolutely entitled to say: 'You're a secretary, John, fuck you.' When what you needed was: 'You're a secretary, John, FUCK YOU.' And then revelling in the pain he was causing.

Gregory Mosher, unpublished interview with
Nesta Jones and Steven Dykes, June 1989

[When Bill Bryden revived his National Theatre production for a limited run at the Mermaid Theatre, the London critics re-affirmed their assessment of the play's position in American theatre history, with Sheridan Morley hailing it as 'an American classic . . . a marvellous latter-day *Death of a Salesman*' (*Punch*, 12 Mar. 1986), and Christopher Edwards also comparing Miller's play, asserting that *Glengarry* 'in its artistry, its strength of writing, and its tautness, is as original a work'

(*The Spectator*, 14 Mar. 1986). In retrospect Bryden, interviewed by Nesta Jones, believed that 'it's the best play about the period' because Mamet 'managed to find a way of explaining Nixon's America, through seven of its citizens, incredibly accurately. It's a wonderful metaphor for the greed and ambitions and the kind of "fuck you Jack" mentality which has been indicative of the Republican ethic from Nixon to the present.' Notable productions of *Glengarry Glen Ross* have also been presented in Canada, South Africa (in Johannesburg and Cape Town) and Australia (in Melbourne, Perth, and Sydney), and in translation in Holland, West Germany, Italy, Switzerland, Denmark, France, Finland, Turkey, Israel, and Japan. The Italian and French critics, particularly, stressed the difficulty of translating Mamet's inimitable language — a point amplified here by Mamet's friend and French translator, Pierre Laville.]

I've seen all eleven productions of *Glengarry* throughout the world. . . . This translation posed an insane problem which would have been impossible to solve without knowing the author. The meaning of every expression and every swearword had to be searched for in order to retain the colour and rhythm of suburban Chicago speech. . . . It's a question of not giving the wrong meanings to the words, of keeping the same shades of sounds, warm and playful, of retaining the rhythm and length of the text. In relation to English, French is not ideal. In order to remain faithful to the American text we even used a metronome and a piano. It took me seven months to translate *Glengarry*.

Pierre Laville, *Pays de Vaud*, 4 Dec. 1986

[The production at the Parco Theatre in Tokyo in Feb. 1989 was so successful that its director Toru Emori, one of Japan's leading actors, mounted a revival at the Haiyuza Theatre in Feb. 1990. In a programme note, the theatre critic Hiroshi Hasebe was concerned to point out the similarities between the business ethics of Japan and America: 'The affluent society that we now enjoy has been supported by these unyielding principles of competition, of capitalism. They are not ideals, we do not wish them, but these facets of reality are the inseparable other sides of ourselves.' In the same programme, Kenji Oba, a Professor at Meiji Gakuin University in Tokyo, commented on the perfect musicality of Mamet's language and the 'ecstacy' it produces in the actor, as 'bold, abusive, obscene words spring forth with splendid rhythm'. He went on to point out the 'soft, flexible, sensitive, and precise' qualities which lie behind the 'roughness' of the male-dominated world of Mamet's plays. He instances the powerful off-stage presence of Levene's daughter, whose illness and needs clearly influence the salesman's motivation.]

It's kind of . . . a bastard play. It's formally a gang comedy in the tradition of *The Front Page* or *Man in White*. And the first act is episodic, almost like a detective story, almost gothic. The second act is a very traditional formal last act of a comedy drama. . . . It's not as good a play as *American Buffalo* — say, for example, by Aristotelian standards . . . and the poetry isn't as good. But I guess it speaks to something that is current in the collective unconscious of the country at this time: the idea of the difference between business and fraud, what's permissible in the name of getting a living and what isn't. . . . But *Glengarry* really isn't a 'whodunnit', it is a gang comedy, which is a play about revealing the specific natures of a bunch of people who happen to be involved in an enterprise.

Mamet, *New Theatre Quarterly*, Feb. 1988

In *Glengarry Glen Ross,* it's interesting to watch Aaranow. He's the one who comes closest to being the character of a raisonneur, for throughout the whole play he's saying, 'I don't understand what's going on', 'I'm no good', 'I can't fit in here', I'm incapable of either grasping those things I should or doing those things which I've grasped'. Or his closing line, 'Oh God, I hate this job.' It's a kind of monody throughout the play. Aaranow has some degree of conscience, some awareness; he's troubled. Corruption troubles him. The question he's troubled by is whether his inability to succeed in the society in which he's placed is a defect — that is, is he manly or sharp enough? — or if it's, in effect, a positive attribute, which is to say that his conscience prohibits him. So Aaranow is left between these two things and he's incapable of choosing. This dilemma is, I think, what many of us are facing in this country right now. As Veblen, who's had a big influence on me, says, a lot of business in this country is founded on the idea that if you don't exploit the possible opportunity, not only are you being silly, but in many cases you're being negligent, even legally negligent.

Mamet, *Studies in American Drama*, 1986

The Shawl

First production: New Th. Company, Briar Street Th., Chicago, 23 Apr. 1985 (dir. Gregory Mosher; with Lindsay Crouse, Mike Nussbaum, and Gary Cole).

First New York production: Lincoln Center Th. Company, Mitzi Newhouse Th., Lincoln Center, 23 Dec. 1985 (dir. Gregory Mosher; with Lindsay Crouse, Mike Nussbaum, and Calvin Levels).

First London production: Th. Upstairs, Royal Court Th., 9 June 1986
(dir. Richard Eyre; with David de Keyser, Connie Booth, and Michael
Feast: recorded for the National Sound Archive).
Notable revivals: New Th., Tel Aviv; Petit Odeon, Paris, Feb. 1989 (dir.
Yves Gasc).
Television: BBC TV, 1989 (dir. Bill Bryden; with Nigel Hawthorne,
Brenda Blethyn, and Karl Johnson).
Published: New York: French, 1985; with *Prairie du Chien*, in *Two
Plays*, New York: Grove, 1985.

---

*John, a phony clairvoyant, is about to con a troubled young
woman, Miss A, out of a fee for advising her in the matter of a
contested will regarding the disposition of her deceased
mother's estate. John's crude young lover is impatient — he
wants thoroughly to cheat the young woman and understand
John's psychic con. John explains how he has either deduced or
researched information that Miss A has construed as mind
reading. But when John finally hooks Miss A with a seemingly
intimate, unknowable detail of her private life, it appears that he
has indeed had a genuine psychic vision.*

[Mamet refers jokingly to *The Shawl* as his episode of *The Twilight
Zone*. He maintains, however, that 'the older guy in *The Shawl* wants to
teach a lesson to his young lover and ends up experiencing a true
psychic vision. . . . The guy is expiating throughout to his young friend.
And what he is saying to the woman, too, is that you cannot overcome
your scepticism because our nature protects us. Finally we have to make
up our own mind about what it is that we have seen (*New Theatre
Quarterly*, Feb. 1988).]

David told me once that he started to write *The Shawl* in part because
people said to him 'You always write such wonderful characters but you
don't write plot'. . . . So he set out to exercise plot-writing as a craft.
And I think it came out beautifully. Everybody gets fooled at least once
in the play. . . . I said to Gregory Mosher one day, 'Let me run my
lines'. . . and it was 'the', 'what', 'in', 'uh', 'ah', 'um'. It's literally
monosyllabic. Even if I have a word, it's part of a sentence that doesn't
exist. On the script it's 'Oh' dot, dot, dot. It's difficult. There are no
arias here. It's more like punchy recitative.

Lindsay Crouse, *New York Times*, 21 Dec. 1985

[The play is written] in that terse elliptical style — replete with interrupted sentences — that is the hallmark of Mamet's writing, but the new element is the suggestion of the supernatural and the mystical, all the more haunting for its quotidian context. Gregory Mosher captures these qualities in a detailed, exacting production, distinguished by Lindsay Crouse, who plays the woman with tough repressed scepticism, and Mike Nussbaum as the medium, a forlorn ironist in baggy pants.

Robert Brustein, *New Republic*, Jan. 1986

[Connie Booth's performance in London as Miss A was universally praised by the critics. John Barber in the *Daily Telegraph* of 11 June 1986 thought that 'her wan intent face' suggested 'a woman with a powerful inner life who is always seeing ghosts at the turn of the stair'. Her brief comment here (from *Drama*, No. 3, 1988), confirms the fascination of Mamet's work for (and the stimulating challenge it offers to) accomplished actors: 'Like Pinter, he demonstrates a superlative ambiguity. It's up to the actor to strip away the layers to reveal what's beneath. The shading has to be just right, the tone completely accurate. In purely technical terms, finding the right way to say something in a Mamet play is like a treasure hunt; there are clues but there are also many incorrect turns you could take.']

[In] *The Shawl* . . . the language of money talks loudest. 'Is this worth money?' asks David de Keyser's John, a charlatan seer who uses mysticism as a kind of coercion. In the part of the seer's victim, Miss A . . . Connie Booth is extremely good. Initially an implacable, diffident presence, she explodes in rage at having been duped — only to realize in an ultimate coup that her debt to John, both emotional and monetary, may be larger than she had envisioned. Michael Feast . . . plays John's assistant, who finds to his horror that his older friend's most avid audience is himself. Neither actor quite masters the Mametian inarticulacy that is this writer's favoured idiom, but Eyre's direction is tacitly voluble — underneath the shawl of language lurk questionable human instincts of which too few American playwrights are courageous to speak.

Matt Wolf, *Plays and Players*, Aug. 1986

The excellent Yves Gasc seems to have . . . understood the elements of fragility, of pain, of ambiguity, in the Pirandellian reflection on the uncertainties of beings and things. . . . Alain Fromanger and Genevieve Casile demonstrate, without superfluous effects, that precariousness, that human powerlessness, the existential evil and distrust of life's illusions which are at the heart of Mamet's work, both as mainspring and conclusion. But . . . we guess at these mysteries, these depths, without quite entering into the landscape painted by the playwright. Something is lacking in order that the adhesion be complete . . . it is doubtless the language.

Pierre Macabru, Le Figaro, 3 Feb. 1989

Prairie du Chien

First production: in the *Earplay* series for National Public Radio, Apr. 1979 (dir: Daniel Freudenberger).

First New York production: with *The Shawl*, Lincoln Center Th. Company, Mitzi Newhouse Th., Lincoln Center, 23 Dec. 1985 (dir. Gregory Mosher).

First London production: with *The Shawl*, Th. Upstairs, Royal Court Th., 9 June 1986 (dir. Max Stafford-Clark: recorded for the National Sound Archive).

Published: in *Short Plays and Monologues*, New York: Dramatists Play Service, 1981; with *The Shawl*, in *Two Plays*, New York: Grove, 1985; London: Methuen, 1989.

Prairie du Chien *began as a radio play, and it unravels on the stage like a Faulkner short story. Set in the lounge car of a railway train, it is essentially a tale told by a cigar-smoking salesman — while a black barman serves drinks and other passengers play gin at a round green card table — about a jealous farmer who stuck a pitchfork in the heart of the black hired hand he found sleeping with his wife, then killed the wife, set fire to the barn, and hanged himself. The sheriff who investigated the affair was himself murdered three years later, after his wife had deserted him, by the father of a ten-year-old girl he had seduced. But this gothic vignette has intriguing supernatural overtones. When men come to investigate the murder of the hired hand, they find no-one in the house except a glowing fawn and a pretty red dress, burning in the closet. Three years later the sheriff himself is discovered in a rocking chair, wearing a red gingham dress and saying 'please help him . . . there in the barn . . . please help him'. The play ends with an outburst of violence on the part of one of the card players, who pulls a gun on the partner he believes to be cheating him.*

Robert Brustein, *New Republic*, Jan. 1986

In *Prairie du Chien*, set in a railway parlour car on a train from Chicago to Duluth in 1910, Nigel Terry plays a compulsive story-teller weaving a Faulknerian shaggy dog story of past violence and conflagration. His tale finds an ironic present-day counterpart in the violence occurring right beside him in the carriage: a card-player ready to kill his opponent over a debt of 87 dollars. 'I'd give a lot to sleep like that', Terry says at the end, referring to the sleeping child in the carriage whose rest has protected him from the surrounding violence. Under Stafford-Clark's unerring direction, the focus suddenly is clear. In a play that could serve as a paradigm of his method, Mamet has given us an enclosed space in which the threat of violence, both voiced and seen, is everywhere palpable.

Matt Wolf, *Plays and Players*, Aug. 1986

Speed-The-Plow

First New York production: Lincoln Center Th. Company, Royale Th., 3 May 1988 (dir. Gregory Mosher; with Joe Mantegna as Bobby Gould, Ron Silver as Charlie Fox, and Madonna as Karen).

First London production: Lyttelton Th., National Th., 25 Jan. 1989 (dir. Gregory Mosher; with Colin Stinton as Gould, Alfred Molina as Fox, and Rebecca Pidgeon as Karen).

Notable revivals: San Niccolo Th., Festival of Two Worlds, Spoleto, 6 July 1988 (dir. Luca Barbareshi); Theater der Freien Volksbuhne, Berlin, 9 Dec. 1988 (dir. Dieter Giesing).

Published: New York: Grove, 1988; London: Methuen 1988; French, 1989; condensed version in *The Best Plays of 1987-1988*, ed. Otis L. Guernsey Jr. and Jeffrey Sweet (New York: Applause, 1989).

Bobby Gould and Charlie Fox, the movie industry sharpies at centre stage, are tribal hustlers in the prize tradition of the penny-ante thieves of American Buffalo, *the low-life real-estate salesmen of* Glengarry Glen Ross, *and the poker playing-conmen of* House of Games. *This time the scam is 'entertainment'. Charlie, a producer, is asking Bobby, a newly appointed head of production, to get approval for a 'package': a big star will do a prison melodrama sure to make a zillion,*

*provided that within 24 hours the studio gives the green light.
No one, of course, actually cares what the commodity is. The
movie's plot, outlined in buzz words, is a riotous morass of
action-and-message-picture clichés that finally must be boiled
down to the single phrase needed to sell it to the studio chief:
'buddy film'. But Mr. Mamet, like his moguls, is not concerned
with the substance of the movie so much as the games that
attend the making of the deal. As Charlie and Bobby, longtime
pals who started out in the mail room together, fantasize about
how much money they are going to make . . . they engage in a
sub rosa power struggle — a warped Pinteresque buddy movie
of their own. . . . Though the men frequently label themselves as
whores, they are sentimental whores who boast of their
brotherly loyalty and describe Hollywood as a 'people business'
even as they stab anyone handy in the back. . . . Yet* Speed-The-
Plow *contains a third character and a second film project —
forces that collide to push Mr. Mamet's drama and themes well
beyond parochial show-biz satire. The catalytic character is a
temporary secretary named Karen. . . . The play's second much
discussed potential film property is* The Bridge, or Radiation and
the Halflife of Society, *a book by an 'Eastern cissy writer' that
an agent has submitted to Bobby's boss.* The Bridge *is the sort
of artsy tome anathema to Hollywood — an allegorical tale of
apocalypse rife with allusions to grace, the fear of death, and
the decay of Western Civilization. Bobby has promised to give
the book a 'courtesy read' before rejecting it, and he also
wouldn't mind taking his temporary secretary to bed. To
accomplish both missions as expeditiously as possible, he gives
Karen the task of preparing a reader's report on the book, with
the hint that the assignment might advance her career to 'the
big table'.*

Frank Rich, New York Times, 4 May 1989

[Even before its Broadway opening, *Speed-The-Plow* generated considerable interest and controversy when it was announced that pop
singer and sometime movie star Madonna would play the part of Karen.
Mamet and Mosher were accused of hatching a cynical publicity stunt,
and some critics questioned the immediate commercial mounting of a
Lincoln Center production, which was initially scheduled as part of the
Center's subscription series. (The announcement of the Broadway

opening with Madonna brought an advanced box office of nearly $750,000 — a record for a 'straight' play.) Madonna's performance became the focus of attention. The majority of the New York critics were gleefully negative about her contribution, but Mamet stands by his choice: 'She didn't unbalance the play. She unbalanced the press. Perhaps it was a tad daring of me.']

Mantegna and Silver are gloriously Mametic; in their hair-trigger, interrupting, overlapping, undercutting exchanges they are in the great tradition of speed-talking actors like Lee Tracy and Pat O'Brien. And Greg Mosher (directing his twelfth Mamet production) propels the action like Howard Hawks at his most kinetic. Mantegna is very funny and then weirdly touching as he moves from a lordly assumption of power to a state of moral confusion. From the man who utters the philosophy of the schlockmeister . . . he becomes the man who says 'I've wasted my life, Charlie, my life is a sham.' Silver's Charlie is the arch-pragmatist, willing to dive to his knees and kiss boss's Rodeo Drive slacks. He accepts Bobby's bastardy, but when the bastard turns virtuous he explodes into a baroque paroxysm of rage that's both hilarious and terrifying. As for Madonna, she has a lot to learn, but she's a serious actress. . . . She doesn't yet have the vocal horsepower, the sparks and cylinders to drive Mamet's syncopated dialogue. But she has the seductive ambiguity that makes Karen the play's catalytic force. This temp can't find the coffee machine, can't punch the right button on the phone, but she can make a Hollywood hardnose throw away eleven years of scheming to follow her into the paths of spiritual redemption. Or is she an even more consummate con artist than the two aces themselves? Madonna hits this chord beautifully, turning her confrontation with Bobby into a double seduction that scrambles all the moral angles. Who better than Madonna — Virgin, Material Girl — to give embodiment to the conundrum at the heart of David Mamet's scathingly comic play?

Jack Kroll, *Newsweek*, May 1988

[The critics were also divided on the nature of the play. Generally it was praised for it's brutally funny satire of Hollywood, but few critics saw the character of the woman as anything other than a girl on the make. The actual contents of *The Bridge* were viewed as mere fodder for parody, and the familiar praise for the playwright's ear was rarely coupled with a serious analysis of the 'ideas contained in the book' or expressed by Karen. It is interesting to note that an unpublished short story written by Mamet in 1978 is also entitled 'The Bridge'. It too deals with an horrific vision of the Apocalypse and contains many of the themes central to such plays as *The Woods* and *Edmond*. A cynical view of Karen as the girl on the make must also be tempered by Mamet's comment that he believed he was writing a latter-day Joan of Arc. The interpretation of the role is clearly an area of some interest — as the comments which follow on the re-casting may suggest.]

Miss [Felicity] Huffman . . . replacing Madonna . . . came close to turning it into a different play, not because of how Madonna performed, but because of how she had been directed. Of the two styles of acting that Mamet fosters — the projection of wild, idiosyncratic plausibility (Mantegna) and the complete absence of any persona (think of the flat, dead, toneless deliveries he elicited from Lindsay Crouse in *House of Games*) — he and Mosher chose the latter for Madonna. In doing so they turned the character into a blank. It didn't really matter that the woman never got her say: we didn't know who she was. Miss Huffman, having studied with Mamet and Macy, is schooled in the technique of projecting a plausible persona, and when she took over the role the woman became an ambiguity rather than a nonentity.

Mimi Kramer, *New Yorker*, 25 Dec. 1989

It's an example of someone trying to be 'the excellent man'. . . . The woman acts as a catalyst . . . she exists as that little irritation that perhaps is able to thrust this man, who is going along in one direction . . . kidding himself, thinking that it's fine: 'I am the excellent man' — yet there's always something nagging at the back of his mind. . . . Then this irritation comes along, this catalyst, this unexpected thing, who throws a mirror in front of him, says: 'It's not okay!'. . . In Bobby Gould, you have a guy who somewhere along the line was a very idealistic person, but who went off . . . and David is the master of that, of writing about people who are in that grey zone. Are they good people? Are they terrible people? I think what David says is that there are no great people, there are no terrible people, it's only grey people: it just depends which side of the grey scale you're looking at. . . . For me, the woman acted as a catalyst, she momentarily prompts his conscience, forces him to go back to the ideals of a five-year-old, of being true to yourself, true to your ideals, but it's such a dangerous and heady position to be in that all it takes is a little nudge back from the other side to give it all up again.

Joe Mantegna, unpublished interview with Nesta Jones and Steven Dykes, Organic Theater, Chicago, May 1989

We were just telling the wrong story the first time out. And this did not occur to me in rehearsal. I thought we were telling that story: a man has to make a decision. He has to chose between unclear and conflicting advice. And that wasn't the story the audience saw at all. They saw the story of a man who had been duped, and the question in the last act became: when will he find out? So the biggest laugh in the show came at the very end when he says: 'I'd like to know the answer.' And the audience was up for grabs, because finally this guy had figured out what we had already figured out half an hour ago. In the second version — this is all directing, mind, nothing to do with acting (except that they're the ones up there, of course) — that line was greeted with silence, as it is in London, as it is in Washington. . . . I think the joy of the play is that it is not, as David would say, a melodrama. It is not a good guy and a bad guy. The people are much more sophisticated. It's a sophisticated telling of a story very similar to *American Buffalo*: the central guy can only believe one person: either the kid is taking drugs or the kid isn't taking drugs. I think it's a better play if the kid isn't taking drugs, but the evidence seems to be that he is. I think *Speed-The-Plow* is a much better play when she's not hustling him, but she might be! But the minute you say in the rehearsal room: 'Well, she is', or even: 'Well, she might be', then the audience tips unalterably to that point of view. So you have to fight for the girl's innocence. . . .

The climax of the play is the girl saying: 'We have a meeting!' And that creates the doubt, because Charlie doesn't have to prove that she's the Whore of Calcutta but that she may not be an angel. The minute that crack is opened you have a moment of reversal; so you want to delay that moment as long as possible. I think everything she says after that is betrayal . . . and he's gone. . . . There's a moment when she calls on God. People call on God a lot in David's plays. . . . And God usually doesn't answer, of course. . . . If you asked David, does he believe in *The Bridge*, he'd say, absolutely. Is it an awkward book? Yes. But the minute the actors have a sense of humour about the book — I don't mean laughing at the book, but having a sense of perspective about it — then the author goes from being a Moonie to being a thoughtful person. . . . The attractiveness of the girl is her integrity, and that's what Charlie realizes he must attack at its source. It's not her behaviour, because her behaviour is understandable in Charlie's terms and in Bobby's higher terms, so he can't fault her for wanting Bobby to make the book, but he can attack her credibility.

Gregory Mosher, unpublished interview
with Nesta Jones and Steven Dykes, 8 June 1989

Watching David Mamet's brilliant *Speed-The-Plow* I was reminded of a line from T. S. Eliot's *Sweeny Agonistes*: 'I gotta use words when I talk to you.' For Mamet's comedy is much more than an anti-Hollywood satire: it is actually, like all Mamet's plays, about the gap between language and feeling, and about the way we use words as a vaporous smoke-screen. Obviously Hollywood, where Mamet had a rough experience with *About Last Night*, provides the mainspring. But just as, in *American Buffalo*, Mamet showed us a group of petty heisters talking big, so here he shows us the new studio brats elevating their tacky deals through self-aggrandizing language. . . . Mamet is not simply settling an old score with Hollywood. What he is saying is that the seats of power are occupied by lonely, frightened, insecure men who use bombast as a defence and who are comically prey to suggestion. . . . That is the core of the play; language as a form of camouflage rather than as a means of communication. . . . Although it might have been more effective in the Cottesloe, Gregory Mosher's production colonizes the big Lyttelton space and gets excellent performances from the cast of three.

Alfred Molina is a particular joy as the would-be big-time Charlie, suggesting a mixture of elephantine greed and naked cunning. He brilliantly balances verbal bluster with, in the last act, a capacity to come up with truth-telling zingers; and, like Dave King in *American Buffalo*, he shows how Mamet benefits from a vaudevillian sense of timing. Colin Stinton is equally impressive as Bobby: he exudes the insolence of office and a brash sexual confidence while suggesting there is something hollow behind the bravura. [As the secretary] Rebecca Pidgeon . . . is all spirituality with a hint of metal.

Michael Billington, *The Guardian*, 26 Jan. 1989

At the National, two of the performers are miscast, and the design and lighting by Michael Merritt and Kevin Rigdon are poor. The settings are of cheap-looking art deco fawn fuzz, with mottled glass screens, and random signs of redecoration — blotches of paint, a step-ladder. But there seem always to be acres of space, dead patches, muzzy long shadows and black spots. . . . [Molina] is a wonderfully vital and appealing actor who sets about Mamet's cascading rhythms and stylistic switchbacks with a real physical vengeance and faultless technique.

Michael Coveney, *Financial Times*, 26 Jan. 1989

Speed-The-Plow is nothing if not a buddy-play. Mamet has always excelled in dramatizing the peculiarly close bonding which occurs between fellow crooks and conmen, showing how their elaborately ritualized professions of loyalty are the comic corollary of profound mutual suspicion. The real conflict is not, it turns out, between art and commerce but between this sort of intense male relationship and a female intruder. . . . Molina and Stinton expertly convey a friendship that has to camouflage its tension in a comedy double act.

Paul Taylor, *The Independent*, 27 Jan. 1989

Greg [Mosher] was asking me which part I wanted to do. He said: 'I assume you want to do the flash part,' as he called it — meaning the part that Fred [Molina] would do. That's the part that had won the Tony Award and the part that comes in and takes over the second act, and it's very showy and flashy, and part of me did want to do that. But, perhaps by virtue of having done Edmond, I just found much more connection with the other part, because he's really the protagonist, and the one who changes and goes through the journey. Most audiences, unfortunately, don't see that, because they get so caught up in the comic story, which is really the story of Charlie Fox: Charlie Fox makes deal, Charlie Fox loses deal, Charlie Fox regains deal — the basic A B A comic structure — and, against impossible odds, in the end he somehow manages to prevail: that's the basic comic story. The tragedy is about the downfall of someone who is lost, who is given the chance of being found and who is lost again. . . . People make an assumption about the play . . . that it's Mamet's revenge on Hollywood. But it's his *advice* to Hollywood: it's a sermon — and just as a sermon accuses its congregation, drawing their attention to the ways in which they have sinned, it is not with the intention of dragging them down, but of aiding them, saving them. . . . He says there are opportunities for salvation and presents them. . . . He says be true to yourself — and Charlie Fox is true to himself. But the idea of Bobby being lost is repeated throughout the play: the opening lines identify what the play is asking — will he or will he not be found —and also identify the battleground on which this will be fought: the conflict between art and entertainment in Movieland. . . . This is his sermon to Hollywood: 'Don't be afraid. Be true to yourself. If you harbour notions of making an important film, a film that makes a difference, a film that is ardent — it may be laughed at, it may be ridiculous, but go ahead and have the guts to do it.' That is what he found when he went out there . . . scared people.

Colin Stinton, unpublished interview with
Nesta Jones and Steven Dykes, July 1989

Bobby Gould in Hell

First production: in a double-bill with Shev Silverstein's *The Devil and Billy Markham*, Mitzi E. Newhouse Th., Lincoln Center, New York, 5 Dec. 1989 (dir. Gregory Mosher; with W. H. Macy, Treat Williams, Felicity Huffman, and Steve Goldstein). *Unpublished.*

Bobby Gould sits waiting in a luxuriously furnished drawing

*room redolent of an exclusive gentlemen's club. Working
studiously at a desk in the corner is the Interrogator's Assistant:
the book into which he writes copious notes is Bobby's 'file'.
This is Hell. Bobby will soon discover that behind the oak-
panelled doors are hidden infernal flames and the terrible
screams of the damned. In a flash of light and cascade of dry
ice, the Interrogator appears, all dressed down to go fishing and
not at all happy at being dragged away from his recreational
activity. Veering wildly from pleasant chit-chat to alarming
conundrums, the Interrogator succeeds in unsettling both Bobby
and his eager-to-please Assistant. Bobby must admit he is a bad
man, but refuses to do so. Glenna, a young woman whom Bobby
had treated badly in a brief relationship, is brought down to the
other world as the prosecution's star witness. But Glenna also
obstinately refuses to play by the Devil's rules. She finds Hell
much as she expected — a bastion of male chauvinism — and
proceeds not only to detail Bobby's shabby behaviour toward
her, but also to upbraid the Interrogator for his 'demeaning'
attitude towards women, suggesting he might benefit from
'counselling'. Eventually, he manages to outwit her and send
her back to her apartment, but will not accept Glenna's
'impossible' personality as an excuse for Bobby's attitude
towards her. Bobby is damned for being 'cruel without being
interesting'. Beneath the witty word-play and startling pyro-
technics, the piece is a simple but chilling morality play. Bobby
is given the chance to return to normal life with the slate wiped
clean, his conscience clear. From now on, he can behave well,
not stray from the path of righteousness. But his cynicism
betrays him: offered the chance to do good, Bobby can only ask,
'But what if I don't? What then?' All too soon, the horror of the
lost opportunity dawns on him. Bobby realizes he has damned
himself, and the Interrogator, his job done, returns to his
fishing. He leaves with a laugh, but it is a laugh less triumphant
than wearily resigned to man's folly. At last truly sorry, Bobby
is informed by the Assistant that he can now go home, and the
Interrogator, planted in the audience, gets to deliver the show's
cracking punchline.*

David came in with this sprawling script. It was brilliant in flashes, and
we sort of knew what it was about. We had a read-through in the theatre

and people working here came to watch. You could see them holding their foreheads. I asked someone after, 'What did you think?' She said, 'I have this awful headache. Oh, not because of the read-through, it's just — er — I — I —', and she would beat a retreat. Well, we all know David is a brilliant writer, but in that first week I have never seen him or anyone show such prowess in theatricality. This huge thing, which was twice as long as it is now, he shaped a play out of it. He just cut everything that wasn't needed — brilliant though it may be. I mean, we're still pissing and moaning about some of the hysterical bits that went. They went because they didn't have anything to do with the throughline. And he'd go away and fax in new bits or revised bits. It's the intellectual flights of fancy that we haven't seen for a while. He takes you up to this intellectual plane and it's like doing a highwire act. You must accept the premise of the play. It's like, 'Do you speak any Swahili at all?' 'A smattering,' 'Okay, I'm going to tell you a joke in Swahili.' And you've got to struggle with the language.

W. H. Macy, unpublished interview with Steven Dykes,
Lincoln Center, New York, 28 Dec. 1989

A juxtaposition of the ordinary with the outlandish lies at the heart of both Mamet's and Silverstein's humour. The movie they wrote together, *Things Change*, was a Mafia thriller couched in the terms of a fairy story, and one naturally assumed that in the division of labour Silverstein — the songwriter, poet for children, and writer of whimsical one-act plays — had provided the fairy-tale element and Mamet the *noir* ambience. The most refreshing thing about *Oh, Hell* is the way each playwright seems to be working in the other's medium. After all, the world of pool halls and con games, where *Billy Markham* takes place, is Mamet's turf, just as obscenity has come to seem his special province. Nearly all the obscenity in *Oh, Hell* belongs to the Silverstein piece, all the whimsy to Mamet. It's as though the two men had agreed to swap souls for a term. . . . Given Mamet's Shavian morality and his sense of tradition, it was a dead cert, really, that one of his heroes would wind up in Hell defending himself to a woman he'd wronged. For the purposes of *Bobby Gould in Hell*, the title character is — like Shaw's Don Juan — the common Enemy of Woman. He's Everycad, and what makes it so comical — such a brilliant casting and directorial coup on Gregory Mosher's part is — to have Gould played here not by the wicked, swift, subtle Joe Mantegna (who created the character in *Speed-The-Plow*) but by Treat Williams, with a look of dumb suffering and the demeanor of a dog who can't understand why he's been put out for the night.

Mimi Kramer, *New Yorker*, 25 Dec. 1989

Gould in Hell is not as tightly written as Mamet's major work, but it is a lovely, silly, smart little piece — filled with typical Mamet double-speak poetic patter. . . . It also has sweet childish jokes (a little Henry Youngman and a man in a bear suit) and terrific flashy magic tricks — a rarity in a production by the usually spare Gregory Mosher. Note, incidentally, it has Mamet's first complex, powerful woman character in a long time, even if the dating humour seems an updated echo of his early *Sexual Perversity in Chicago.* Perhaps best of all, it has a role for Macy that puts him up where he has always belonged, with such top Mamet players as Mantegna and Mike Nussbaum. Macy's Devil is bliss incarnate — an erratic, moody, ironic fellow who gets impatient with stupidity but isn't too blasé for a decent revelation.

Linda Winer, *Newsday*, 6 Dec. 1989

b: Short Plays and Monologues

Litko

Dramatic monologue, written as a companion piece to *Duck Variations.*
First production: New Room at the Body Politic Th., Chicago, 1972,
   (dir. David Mamet; with Jim Brett).
Published: in *Short Plays and Monologues*, New York: Dramatists Play
   Service, 1981; and in *Goldberg Street*, New York: Grove, 1985.

A dissertation on the nature of theatre, performed by an actor in the style of a Las Vegas stand-up comedian.

All Men are Whores

First production: Yale Cabaret, Feb. 1977 (dir. David Mamet; with Patti
   Lupone, Kevin Kline, and Sam Tsoutsovas).
Notable revivals: Chicago, 27 June 1984 (dir. Jim Wise); Vienna
   English Th., 22 Sept. 1985 (dir. Edward Albee).
Published: in *Short Plays and Monologues*, New York: Dramatists Play
   Service, 1981; and in *Goldberg Street*, New York: Grove, 1985.

In seventeen scenes, Sam, Kevin, and Patti take turns addressing the audience. Their talk is of sexual experience, of failed, half-forgotten relationships: erotic, loving, brutal, and perverse. Sam feigns a cynical, almost clinical, disinterest in his acknowledgement that people 'will do anything for some affection', but it is he who seems nearest breaking point. Kevin is single, promiscuous, and confused. His recollections of past affairs are romantic and sensual, but undermined by a bitterness verging on misogyny. Patti — at first all accommodation and encouragement — rapidly despairs of the complexities of sex and the pathological fears of men. The style of the piece is confrontational, yet never loses the intimacy of a shared moment.

I wrote a play once called *All Men Are Whores*, and in it a guy said that men are the puppy dogs of the universe and that they'll do anything for some affection. Especially in this country, men are never forced to confront themselves, and so they have no rock-bottom self-respect. We'll do anything to get some, because we feel there's nothing that can be taken from us. We've learned to define ourselves solely in terms of our work, and in an economy that's crumbling and where there's no certainty, what's left?

You know, a whorehouse is ostensibly a place to have a heterosexual experience, but it's really a homosexual experience, because it has to do with proclaiming yourself in terms of other men. And a whorehouse is the way straight men see America. Women have, in men's minds, such a low place on the social ladder in this country that it's useless to define yourself in terms of a woman. What men need is men's approval.

Men need to love in a hierarchical situation. Whoever fucks the eighteen-year-old has self-respect for tonight. Or, there are ten jobs in the room. Whoever gets the highest job gets the Cadillac.

Mamet, *Vogue*, July 1984

Dark Pony

First production: Yale Repertory Th., New Haven, Conn., 14 Oct. 1977 (dir. Walt Jones; with Lindsay Crouse and Michael Higgins).

First New York production: Circle Repertory, 18 Oct. 1979 (dir. Mamet; with Lindsay Crouse and Michael Higgins).

First London production: King's Head Th. Club, Feb. 1981 (dir. Stuart Owen; with Don and Susannah Fellowes).

Published: in *Two Plays*, New York: Grove, 1979; and in *Three Plays*.

Dark Pony *is a subtle, lyrical, dreamlike vignette that runs about five minutes. . . . In it, a father tells his five-year-old daughter a story about an Indian boy and his pony. The action takes place in the front seat of their car as they drive home. The child knows the story and can therefore listen to the car drive over the pavement. When the sound of the pavement changes, she knows they're near home. The story ends. It's a lovely little tale about childhood memories and emotions.*

Mike Steele, *Star Tribune* (Minneapolis), 21 Jan. 1978

Mr. Happiness

First production: Plymouth Th., New York, 6 Mar. 1978 (dir. Steven Schachter).

Notable revivals: Radio Telefis Eireann, 10 Sept. 1984; Haymarket Th., Leicester, 27 Oct. 1987 (dir: Scott Antony; with Brian Jackson); Platform Performance, National Th., London, June 1986 (with Colin Stinton).

Published: in *Two Plays*, New York: Grove, 1978.

A short, ironic monologue, written as a complementary piece for the Broadway opening of The Water Engine. *Mr. Happiness, a radio personality of the 'thirties, solves his listeners' problems over the air.*

A Sermon

First production: Apollo Th., Chicago, 16 Jan. 1979 (dir. Sheldon Patinkin; with Cosmo White and, later, W. H. Macy).

Notable revivals: Ensemble Studio Th., 24 Aug. 1981 (dir. Mamet; with David Rasche); Festival of the Two Worlds, Spoleto, July 1987 (with Luca Barbareschi); Platform Performance, National Th., London, Mar. 1989 (with Colin Stinton).

Published: in *Short Plays and Monologues*, New York: Dramatists Play Service, 1981; and in *Goldberg Street*, New York: Grove, 1985.

A one-actor journey through stray thoughts that are ridiculous and yet right to the point, non-sequiturs and wisdoms merged.

The form is foolishness: a hip sort of speaker . . . playfully deals with themes of life and love, foibles and fatuities. But the aim is serious.

Peter P. Jacobi, *Christian Science Monitor*, 23 Feb. 1979

The Blue Hour: City Sketches

First production: Public Th., New York, Feb. 1979 (workshop production, dir. Mamet; with Ben Halley Jr., David Sabin, Arthur French, Patti Lupone, Lindsay Crouse, and Colin Stinton).
Published: in *Short Plays and Monologues*, New York: Dramatists Play Service, 1983; and in *Goldberg Street*, New York: Grove, 1985.

American Twilight The prologue: spoken by a man, it describes a winter's evening in the big city, as rush hour fades into 'blue hour'.

Doctor A woman berates her doctor for his callous attitude towards his long-suffering patients and his astronomical charges for treatment.

The Hat A woman and a sales assistant take the time to find the perfect outfit for the customer's important interview.

Businessmen Grey and Black are sat next to one another on a plane. They talk of a restaurant both frequent, and Grey reminisces about his army days outside Chicago and his adventures in the city on leave. The conversation is short and polite. The men soon get back to their work.

Cold Unlike *Businessmen*, where the dialogue remains formal, here the converstaion between two men waiting for a train oversteps the boundary set between strangers, and one of the men eventually turns on the other.

Epilogue In a single line, a man describes the transition of the 'blue hour' into night.

The Sanctity of Marriage

First production: Circle Repertory Th. Company, New York, 18 Oct. 1979 (dir. Mamet; with Lindsay Crouse and Michael Higgins).

A married couple, breaking up, remember a holiday in Europe.

Shoeshine

First production: in *The Invitational: a Celebration of the One-Act Play*, Ensemble Studio Th., New York, 14 Dec. 1979 (dir. W. H. Macy; with Colin Stinton).

Published: in *Short Plays and Monologues*, New York: Dramatists Play Service, 1983; and in *Goldberg Street*, New York: Grove, 1985.

In a scene that lasts little longer than a 'shine', Sam, a middle-aged black man, and his young assistant, Jim, serve their white customers in 'Sam's Shoeshine Parlor'. Two executives enter and discuss business while Sam and Jim go to work. The businessmen's conversation provides a constant backing to the dramatic action of the piece: a customer accuses Jim of stealing his wallet and threatens to call the police. The sketch cleverly syncopates the different rhythms of the very different individual voices of these men. It is a deceptively simple depiction of class, colour, prejudice, and occupation in the big city.

Five Unrelated Pieces

First production: in *Marathon 1983, Festival of One-Act Plays*, Ensemble Studio Th., New York, May 1983 (dir: Curt Dempster).

Published: in *Goldberg Street*, New York: Grove, 1985.

Two Conversations: One Two bourgeois couples discuss the mental breakdown of a cleaner that one couple has recommended to the other.

Two Conversations: Two Two men discuss the complexities of the New Testament, and conclude that it is an account of man's conflict with his homosexual feelings for God the Father.

Two Scenes: One Two men conduct an entire conversation using only numbers as a form of communication. The actual situation remains a mystery.

Two Scenes: Two An aerobics coach takes a class through a work-out.

Yes But So What One man complains of his wife, of his desire to meet with other women, and the guilt inherent in his frustration and rage. His companion sympathizes, and the conversation turns to what is morally right and wrong.

The Disappearance of the Jews

First production: Goodman Th., Chicago, 3 June 1983 (dir. Gregory Mosher; with Joe Mantegna and Norman Parker).
Published: with *Goldberg Street* and *The Luftmensch*, in *Three Jewish Plays*, New York: French, 1987.

The Disappearance of the Jews *shows two ageing Jewish men reminiscing about life back then and life now. They never move from their chairs, but the vignette is so sensitively portrayed by eye, inflection, and intonation that it is far from static. . . . It's a universal and very funny situation. But it is also very sad because as [Mamet] . . . catches the discrepancies of their memories, we see two men growing old and somewhat scared. The wistful aroma of what might have been creeps in, as does the need for the comfort of family elders, the desire to embrace their roots, and the disappointed confessions of how it is now, in fantasy and in reality.*

Glenna Syse, *Chicago Sun-Times*, 15 June 1983

The Dog, Film Crew, *and* Four AM

First production: in *Three by Three*, 'Jason's', Park Royal Hotel, New York, 14 July 1983 (dir. Joe Cacau).
Published: in *Goldberg Street*, New York: Grove, 1985.

The Dog Short monologue in which the speaker recounts the successful house-training of his 'best friend'.

Film Crew Mike and Joe are part of a film unit with time on their hands. Joe eagerly explains the rules of a card game to their dubious fellow-worker Mike. Joe can hardly wait to initiate Mike into the rudiments of the game before he inveigles his victim with: 'Do you want to try a practice hand?'

Four AM   A late night 'talk radio' disc jockey gets a call from a fan who would like to use the broadcast to publicize his organization's plan 'to bring dead people back to life on Jupiter'.

Vermont Sketches

First production: in *Marathon 1984, Festival of One-Act Plays*,
   Ensemble Studio Th., New York, 24 May 1984 (dir. Gregory
   Mosher; with W. H. Macy, Colin Stinton, Frank Hamilton, and Joe
   Ponazecki).
Published: in *Goldberg Street*, New York: Grove, 1985.

Conversations with the Spirit World   Morris and James relate tales of local ghosts. Both men are genuinely disturbed by supernatural phenomena and admit that there are 'places in the woods' where they don't like to go.

Pint's a Pound the World Around   A local merchant is outlining to another the advantages of linking up with a large corporate supplier. He is really trying to persuade himself of the wisdom of such a move.

Dowsing   Two older men, in a Vermont country store, discuss the ancient art of dowsing — the search for underground water or minerals using a forked stick which dips when these are present.

Deer Dogs   Bunchy is trying to convince Larry of the disadvantages of a law which states that any dog suspected of chasing deer can be shot on sight. Larry remains adamant that the law should be strictly enforced.

[*In the Mall*, *Maple Sugaring*, and *Morris and Joe* remain unperformed.]

Goldberg Street

First production: New Th. Company, WNVR Radio, Chicago, 2 Mar.
   1985 (dir. Mamet; with Mike and Susan Nussbaum).
Published: in *Goldberg Street*, New York: Grove, 1985; and in *Three
   Jewish Plays*, New York: French, 1987.

Goldberg Street, *which ran about eight minutes, is a mournful meditation on war, isolation, and Jewish self-hate as experienced by a Jewish man who tells his daughter of his return to a town in France where he fought during the Second World War.*

> Lloyd Sachs, *Chicago Sun-Times*, 6 Mar. 1985

Cross Patch

First production: New Th. Company, WNVR Radio, Chicago, 4 Mar. 1985 (dir. Mamet; with W. H. Macy, Mike Nussbaum, Peter Riegert, and Colin Stinton).
Published: in *Goldberg Street*, New York: Grove, 1985.

Cross Patch, *the title of which is taken from a Mother Goose rhyme, is a twenty-minute visitation to an assembly hall in which a succession of men who like the sound of their own voices — military and bureaucratic types — give 'rousing' speeches on patriotism, the entrepreneurial spirit, and the link between God, money, and force.*

> Lloyd Sachs, *Chicago Sun-Times*, 6 March 1985

The Spanish Prisoner

First production: New Th. Company, Briar Street Th., Chicago, 23 April 1985 (dir. Gregory Mosher; with Peter Riegert and Sheila Welch).
Published: in *Goldberg Street*, New York: Grove, 1985.

The play is an intense dialogue divided into three trains of thought or argument. The first has to do with the idea of 'personality' — how the earth's natural tendency towards rest or decay is forever opposed by man's force of personality. If, as the more dominant character argues, 'Balance, as a basic principle of nature, is attractive', why do we constantly seek to overthrow natural order? The second phase is a more lateral discussion concerning the sinking of a Spanish galleon, and finally, inspired by the report of a black youth killed in Alabama, the two pontificate on the fate of the world had the boy lived.

[*Food*, *Columbus Avenue*, *Steve McQueen*, *Yes*, *In Old Vermont*, and *The Power Outage*, published in *Goldberg Street* (New York: Grove, 1985), and *The Luftmensch*, published in *Three Jewish Plays* (New York: French, 1987), remain unperformed, as does *Dodge*, published in *Harper's Magazine* in 1989.]

c: Adaptations

Red River
from the play by Pierre Laville.

First production: Goodman Th., Chicago, 2 May 1983 (dir. Robert Woodruff). *Unpublished.*

The play. . . covers sixteen crucial years (1924-40) in the history of the Soviet Union. . . . Its central character is Mikhail Bulgakov, the Russian writer whose plays and novels were banned in his lifetime (1891-1940) and are only now becoming more widely known. Running parallel with his life . . . is the story of Mayakovsky, the futurist poet who, censured for his writings after a life of dedication to the brave new world he envisioned in Soviet Russia, committed suicide in 1930. Involved in minor roles are such historical figures as the director Stanislavsky and the dictator Josef Stalin. Laville's central theme is the crushing of the creative individual spirit by totalitarian forces. His tragic hero, Bulgakov, begins with the joyful knowledge that his novels will be read; but the play ends with the writer buried in obscurity.

Richard Christiansen, Chicago Tribune, 3 May 1983

The Cherry Orchard
from the play by Chekhov, based on a literal translation by Peter Nelles.

First production: New Th. Company, Goodman Th. Studio, 15 Mar. 1985 (dir. Gregory Mosher; with Lindsay Crouse, Colin Stinton, Peter Riegert, W. H. Macy, Mike Nussbaum, and Linda Kimborough). *Published:* New York: Grove, 1985.

Chekhov's time is very analagous to the period we live in now. When you look at *The Cherry Orchard*, it is almost an accurate prediction of the coming of the Soviet era. The aristocracy could no longer support itself. That it would be replaced by a new order was inevitable. There was a vast upheaval afoot. Something was going to happen. And today we all feel something is going to happen in our world. We don't know any more than Chekhov knew, but obviously things are not going to continue as they have for much longer. There is some greater force at work in our lives, a force so great we cannot fully perceive it, but we know it is there. . . . My contribution to this production is described by the awkward word 'adaptation'. Chekhov wrote the play. Peter Nelles . . . rendered it into English. I took Nelles's work and tried to choose between the alternate word meanings where he supplied them, and to adapt the literal meanings into rhythmic, dramatic prose.

Mamet, *Chicago Sun-Times*, 3 Mar. 1985

[Mamet believes that 'the title is a flag of convenience. Nobody in the play gives a damn about the cherry orchard'. The play is 'a series of scenes about sexuality, and in particular, frustrated sexuality'. Mosher shares this view describing the play as 'a love story'. When asked for some further clues to his interpretation, Mosher repeated one of his favourite Mamet quotes: 'We are all ready to pay the price. The problem is it's always exacted in some currency we did not expect.']

Vint

From the short story by Chekhov (one of seven such dramatizations, commissioned by John Houseman. His Acting Company undertook a Sixty Cities Tour of the seven plays, presented under the collective title, *Orchards*.)
First production: Kannert Center, University of Illinois, Sept., 1985 (dir. Robert Falls).
Published: in *Orchards*, New York: Broadway Play Publishing, 1987.

A high-ranking bureaucrat happens upon four of his subordinates playing Vint (a card game) at the office late one night. In place of cards the four men play with identity dossiers — various departments are counted as suits, ranks are given denominational status. The Commissioner is outraged to overhear his wife being bidded upon and taken in a trick, but soon he warms to the metaphor and ends up joining in the game.

Uncle Vanya

from the play by Chekhov, based on a literal translation by Vlada
   Chernomordik.
First production: American Repertory Th. at the Hasty Pudding Th.,
   Cambridge, Mass., 16 April 1988 (dir. David Wheeler; with Lindsay
   Crouse and Christopher Walken).
Published: New York: Grove, 1989.

[The adaptation was commissioned by Robert Brustein, who considers
that Mamet has created 'an act of deconstruction designed to exhume the
living energies of Chekhov's writing from under the heavy weight of
"masterpiece topsoil".' The director, David Wheeler, found that Mamet
made the play 'a very contemporary piece, very sharp and very funny',
the language becoming 'informal and fluent, instead of formal and
literary. During rehearsals all the actors remarked on how easy it was to
memorize their lines, because their lines sounded so much like the way
people really talk. Mamet has an interest in language as it comes from
an actor's mouth, which is critical for comedy' (*Boston Campus Calendar*, Apr. 1988).

d: Children's Plays

The Poet and the Rent

'A Play for Kids from Seven to 8:15.'
First production: St. Nicholas Th. Company, June 1975 (dir. W. H.
   Macy).
Notable revival: Lahden Kaupingin Teatteri Lahti, Finland, 4 Feb. 1988.
Published: New York: French, 1981; and in *Three Children's Plays*,
   New York: Grove, 1986.

The Revenge of the Space Pandas
or Binky Rudich and the Two-Speed Clock

First production: St. Clement's Th. Company, Flushing Town Hall,
   New York, June 1977 (dir. Matthew Elk).

Notable revivals: St. Nicholas Th., Nov. 1977 (dir. Steven Schachter).
Published: in *Three Children's Plays*, New York: Grove, 1986.

The Frog Prince

First production: as a staged reading at the Goodman Th., Chicago,
   17 May 1982 (with Linda Kimborough and Jack Wallace).
Notable revival: O'Malley Th., Roosevelt University, Chicago, 7 Dec.
   1989 (dir. Susan Nussbaum).
Radio production: Atlantic Th. Company, Vermont, 1989 (dir. Mamet).
Published: New York: French, 1983; and in *Three Children's Plays*,
   New York: Grove 1986.

Compilers' Note

Over the last twenty years, Mamet has maintained a considerable output
of new and adapted plays, but inevitably some interesting projects have
failed to materialize — such as the projected dramatization of Theodore
Dreiser's *An American Tragedy*, which had been scheduled for production at the National Theatre, London, in 1979. It should also be noted
that several of Mamet's short plays, although performed, remain unpublished, including *Mackinac*, *Marranos*, and *Where Were You When It
Went Down?* (for all of which, see Chronology), and a piece entitled
Addiction, specially written for a benefit for new writers at the West
Side Arts Theater, New York, in 1985. And the following short pieces
all await a first production: *LA Sketches, The Museum of Science and
Industry, Donny March* (a moving monologue in which a woman talks
to her child), *Almost Done*, and an intriguing late-night conversation
between a man and his daughter-in-law entitled *Joseph Dintenfass*.

The Films

Mamet made his screenwriting debut with *The Postman Always Rings Twice* (Lorimer Pictures, 1981), an adaptation of James M. Cain's novel (1934). Bob Rafelson, the film's director, and Mamet both acknowledged Cain as a major influence on their own work and held each other's in high regard. From the outset Rafelson was concerned to involve Mamet in all aspects of production, providing him with the opportunity to gain first-hand experience of film-making; and Mamet recognized through this collaboration the debt he owed to Rafelson in teaching him the craft of screenwriting. The partnership was, however, only partially successful: their brooding, brutally erotic vision of the novel which paired Jack Nicholson and Jessica Lange as Cain's murderous lovers, divided critical opinion and the film did not do well at the box office. Nevertheless, Mamet's screenplay did receive some favourable notices, and he was largely enthusiastic about his first Hollywood venture. Moreover, his work on *Postman* was to have an immediate effect on his next theatre piece: 'Cain's beautiful vision . . . is about killing and screwing and betraying each other — and under all this very cynical vision is a crying need for human contact in a bad, bad world' (Mamet, *Film Comment*, April 1981) — a perfect description of the themes he was about to tackle in *Edmond*.

Mamet's second film, *The Verdict* (Columbia Pictures, 1982), teamed him with another outstanding director, Sidney Lumet. Based on a novel by Barry Reed, the story follows Paul Newman as a drunken, ambulance-chasing lawyer on his 'road to Damascus'. Hailed as 'certainly one of the finest courtroom movies ever made . . . with some of the best dialogue heard on the screen this year' (David Denby, *New York*, 20 Dec. 1982), *The Verdict* was duly nominated for an Academy Award for Best Adapted Screenplay. Such was the film's success that Lumet and Mamet initiated another collaborative project: a screen version of *The Autobiography of Malcolm X*. Mamet spent a year adapting the book, but initial interest from Warner Brothers waned, and the screenplay (Nov. 1983) remains unproduced.

Mamet's disenchantment with Hollywood came with *About Last Night* (RCA, 1986), purportedly based on *Sexual Perversity in Chicago*. Mamet sold the film rights in the late 'seventies, presenting his own screenplay to the producers. But they, determined to maximize the commercial potential of the work, fired Mamet, brought in their own writers, and cast solid box-office favourites in the four leading roles. The film succeeds in perverting the intention of the original play and Mamet disassociated himself from the entire project.

The Untouchables (Paramount, 1987), an epic reworking of the popular TV series from the 'fifties, tells the tale of the four incorruptible law officers who brought down Al Capone's Empire of Crime in the Chicago of the prohibition era. Mamet was delighted at the chance to recreate the glorious myths of his home town, and his screenplay is a large-scale, wide-ranging vision of gangster lore, matched by Brian de Palma's flamboyant direction. There are shoot-outs, gangland slaughters, and courtroom melodramatics, but 'despite its driving pace, style, and wit, this film's pervasive mood is a strange and haunting sadness' (Richard Schickel, *Time Magazine*, 8 June 1987). Mamet was keen that an audience should find the central relationship between Eliot Ness (Kevin Costner) and the old Irish cop (Sean Connery), who teaches him to fight Capone with dignity, 'moving'. Nevertheless, as in much of Mamet's work, it is the Devil who gets the best tunes, and Robert De Niro's performance as Al Capone fuels the film's most powerful moments. The now famous 'Baseball Bat' scene is as much an illustration of Mamet's art as it is a display of De Niro's chilling power or De Palma's dramatic manipulation of the camera: 'Like any gangster picture, it's a myth about good and evil — the attractiveness of evil and the triumph of good. The aspects of Capone's character I try to bring out are his absolute charm and his absolute viciousness' (Mamet, *Chicago Tribune*, 21 Sept. 1986).

The Untouchables proved a popular and critical success, but even before its completion Mamet's attention had turned to his next project, *House of Games*, which marked his directorial debut. Based on a story that Mamet and his college friend, Jonathan Katz, had devised years before, *House of Games* (Orion, 1987) received almost universal praise on its release and soon attained the status of a cult classic: 'Mamet has made a "film noir" for the 'eighties, a subversive under-the-rock look at the interlocking scams that define much of today's moral universe' (Jack Kroll, *Newsweek*, 19 Oct. 1987). The *Los Angeles Weekly* (23 Oct. 1987) accused Mamet of a mysoginistic pleasure in tormenting his heroine under 'the pretext of giving his tale a progressive, feminist significance', but Kroll felt that Lindsay Crouse 'with poignant intelligence and stark, clean technique created a classic portrait' of Dr. Margaret Ford, a woman much darker and more complex than the traditional 'Hitchcock victim'. Ford's Nemesis, the shady con-man, Mike, is played by Joe Mantegna: 'He knows what she is as soon as he meets her. He knows that she needs something, is searching for something. They are the same person, really. But he tells the truth, she doesn't. There's a point beyond which he will not go. She ventures into other areas.' These 'areas' are what the film so effectively explores and which lead to its violent climax. Margaret's life is drastically altered: 'Mike changes her life. At the end of the film she is dressed beautifully, her hair all done, she is smiling. It takes years of therapy to achieve what Mike gives her in a week-end' (unpublished interview with Nesta Jones and Steven Dykes, 28 May 1989).

Understandably anxious as a first-time director, Mamet surrounded himself on the set with colleagues from his work in the theatre. This production team — including designers Michael Merritt and Nan Cibula, musician Alaric Jans, and actors from the St. Nicholas and Goodman companies — also formed the core of Mamet's next feature, *Things Change* (Columbia, 1988). Co-written with Shel Silverstein and produced (like *House of Games*) by Michael Hausman, the film is a 'Mafia fairy tale', in which an elderly shoeshine man (Don Ameche) is mistaken for a Mafia big shot. The comedy is gentle, almost melancholy: 'Mamet's cagey, coiled playwright prose is on holiday here, but you are unlikely to miss it. Instead, you share the pleasure he takes in spinning a favourite old tale in the shank of a lazy back-room evening with the boys' (Richard Corliss, *Time*, 24 Oct. 1988). There is a moral, but Mamet does not push it: 'It's a fable about frustrated ambition. A fable is a gentle myth that treats common human problems in an elevated way so that we can see them for what they are without being frightened by them' (Mamet, *Observer Magazine*, Jan. 1989).

Mamet's final contribution to film in the 'eighties was his reworking of an old Humphrey Bogart/Warner Brothers gangster comedy *We're No Angels* (Paramount, 1989), with Robert De Niro and Sean Penn playing a pair of escaped convicts mistaken for celebrated priests. Neil Jordan, the director, described the screenplay as one of the best he had ever read. Curiously, the prospect of a film combining the prodigious talents of Mamet, Jordan, and De Niro failed to live up to its promise. Most critics found it frustrating: '*We're No Angels* has to be the most overqualified comedy of the year. . . . Needless to say the film is extremely stylish . . . [but] it's a style utterly at odds with Mamet's foursquare, old fashioned situational comedy: it kills the joke. Though Penn and a heavily mugging De Niro earn their share of chuckles, you leave this comedy scratching your head at the nutty incongruity of the endeavour' (David Ansen, *Newsweek*, 25 Dec. 1989).

Perhaps the most interesting of Mamet's recent film projects is *Homicide* (1989), now in production for Bison Films. After the whimsy of *Things Change* and *We're No Angels*, this violent depiction of life in the Chicago police department comes as something of a shock — a controversial thriller focusing on racial tensions within the force and the city. *Homicide* is the first of Mamet's screenplays to deal specificially with issues concerning contemporary Chicago, and the dialogue is a powerful distillation of street language and 'copspeak'. Mamet, who is directing the film himself, is unashamedly ambitious for the project: 'The solution to this case is gonna define the nature of evil. . . . It's a difficult script' (*Time Out*, Dec. 1988). Mamet also contributed an episode to the TV series *Hill Street Blues*: entitled 'A Wasted Weekend', it was first transmitted by NBC on 13 Jan. 1987.

In the last decade Mamet has emerged as one of the most innovative and idiosyncratic of film-makers. Several accounts of his experiences as a writer in Hollywood and as a director on the set of his own films appear in *Writing in Restaurants* and *Some Freaks*. He also plans to publish a study of film directing and writing based on his seminars with film students at Columbia University. Three of his screenplays have been published — *House of Games* (New York: Grove, 1987; London: Methuen, 1988), *Things Change*, written with Shel Silverstein (New York: Grove, 1988), and *We're No Angels* (New York: Grove Weidenfeld, 1990).

Collections of Essays

Writing in Restaurants. New York: Viking Penguin, 1986; London: Faber, 1988.
Some Freaks. New York: Viking Penguin, 1989; London: Faber 1990.
    [For further particulars of both volumes, see Section 5, p. 94, below.]

Poetry

The Hero Pony, forthcoming.

Books for Children

The Owl, with Lindsay Crouse. Kipling Books, 1987.
Warm and Cold, with illustrations by Donald Sultan. New York: Fawbush/Solo, 1985; Grove, 1988. ['A poetic depiction of what keeps you warm when it is cold, from good clothes and steam to the sound of talk and the love that you keep with you wherever you go.']

I was raised in a typically American environment. My parents were not interested in preserving their European heritage and were enthusiastic in their complete dedication to the materialistic values of American society. At home everything was defined negatively: let's stop being poor, let's stop being Russian, let's stop being Jews. I mean, all these three terms together give most Americans a substantial headache, right? And that abandonment of any sense of community and collective social goals depresses and frightens me.

Time Out, November 1986

I came to New York to study acting at the Neighborhood Playhouse, a school of theatre where I came back later to work as an actor and director. I kind of stumbled upon a career as a playwright. I became a playwright because I was an actor and I started directing because I wasn't a very good actor and I started writing because I was working with very young actors and there was nothing for them to do.

New Theatre Quarterly, February 1988

Pinter was probably the most influential when I was young and malleable . . . *The Homecoming*, *The Basement*, especially the revue sketches. I felt a huge freedom because of Pinter's sketches — to deal in depth and on their own merit with such minutiae.

Drama, No. 3, 1988

To me, a writer has to write. Really, the only tool he has is the dialogue and the absolutely essential minimal stage directions; the rest of the staging must be the province of the director. What the characters say to each other must contain and give birth to what they do to each other. There are always attempts to get away from that, but you can't, because every time you do, you end up with garbage. There are always trends, but basically there's nothing new in theatre. It always has been, and always will be, just actors and audiences, no matter how many fucking lazers you put in. You can't get beyond the beauty of actors on a stage. Nothing will make that more beautiful if they're correct, and nothing will save that if they're incorrect. . . . What I'm saying is that experimentation is, *per se*, a non-regenerative idea; it has to be experimentation related to what the script says about ourselves, and how best to achieve that. A different kind of experimentation, which is crap, is: 'How do we use this technology?' Who cares? I'm not saying that technology is out of place in theatre; I'm saying it has no intrinsic value. It's most times a distraction.

New York Arts Journal, Feb-March 1978

My real concern always is with the play as a whole; with writing the play. There's a curious phenomenon that happens when you compose a play or movie. The creation very quickly takes on a life of its own. I have no idea why; it's just words on paper. But the art I can compare it to in my experience is carving wood. You start to carve wood and very quickly the thing takes on a life of its own. Part of the wisdom of wood carving is to realize when the wood is telling you where it wants to go. Obviously it's going to be a duck if you start out to make a duck, but the kind of duck it's going to be is largely dictated by the kind of wood. And there is a similar phenomenon in writing drama. You start out with an idea, it becomes something else, and part of the wisdom is learning to listen to the material itself. . . .

I'm sure trying to do the well-made play. It is the hardest thing to do. I like this form because it's the structure imitating human perception. . . . This is the way we perceive a play: with a clear beginning, a middle, and an end. . . . So when one wants to best utilize the theatre, one would try to structure a play in a way that is congruent with the way the mind perceives it. Everybody wants to hear a story with a beginning, middle, and end. . . . The language in my plays is not realistic but poetic. The words sometimes have a musical quality to them. It's language which is tailor-made for the stage. People don't always talk the way my characters do in real life, although they may use some of the same words. Think of Odets, Wilder. That stuff is not realistic; it is poetic. It's not a matter, in *Lakeboat or Sexual Perversity in Chicago* or *Edmond* or my other plays, of my 'interpretation' of how these people talk. It is an illusion.

Studies in American Drama, 1986

My plays don't really call for, nor will they support, a lot of invention. I always think of something Stanislavsky said — that any director who has to do something interesting with the text does not understand the text. So that would be my dictum, along with Stanislavsky. Don't be 'interesting'. If you are doing Shakespeare, it does not make any difference if you put it in evening dress or the Wild West to the audience's enjoyment of the play. Because what they're following are the actions of the characters.

New Theatre Quarterly, February 1988

The purpose of the theatre is not primarily to deal with social issues; it's to deal with spiritual issues. . . . I think the purpose of theatre is not to deepen the mysteries of life, but to celebrate the mysteries of life. That's what a good play does, and that's what a good play has done for ten thousand years.

The only person who can get what he wants is the individual man. You can't do it as a race; you can't do it as a culture. In the theatre an individual has to come to terms with what he wants and how capable he is of getting it. Making peace with the gods — that's what drama's all about.

South Carolina Review, 1985

[Theatre is] an essential part of our lives. We tell stories all the time. We go to the theatre to hear stories told just like we tell them to each other. In our interaction in our daily lives we tell stories to each other, we gossip, we complain to each other, we exhort. These are means of defining what our life is. The theatre is a way of doing it communally, of sharing that experience, and it's absolutely essential.

Washington Post, 25 August 1983

American drama is just taking the same direction that American culture is taking. I mean, it would be rather surprising if we had a flourishing, happy theatre in this country. . . . In a very, very strictly structured, increasingly authoritarian environment, which is life in this country, if one pursues a career one of the main aspects of which is being an iconoclast, one is not going to have the happiest time of it. . . . I don't think I am a political playwright. I think I probably have as good a chance of ending up in jail as anybody else, but I don't think I am a political playwright. . . . Tearing down the icons of American business and some of the myths about this country. This is one of the jobs of the writer.

If people like everything you do, then you are doing something wrong, I believe. That is especially true if you are rather prolific, as I am. People sometimes find it hard to make an honest evaluation of your plays based on objective critical standards. They would be horrified to assume that the vast majority of what I write, taken as a body, can be any good, because there is too much of it. This is one of the down sides of being prolific. . . . Some people are going to like one kind of play, some are going to like another. Some are going to overlap, but no one is going to like all of them.

New Theatre Quarterly, February 1988

a: Primary Sources

Bibliographic details of individual plays and adaptations will be found under their titles in Section 2, and of published filmscripts and other non-dramatic writing in Section 3.

Collections of Plays

Three Plays: American Buffalo, Sexual Perversity in Chicago, and *Duck Variations.* London: Methuen, 1978.

Dramatic Sketches and Monologues. New York: French, 1985. [Contains *Five Unrelated Pieces, The Power Outage, The Dog, Film Crew, Four AM, Food, Pint's a Pound the World Around, Deer Dogs, Columbus Avenue, Two Scenes, Conversations with the Spirit World, Maple Sugaring, Morris and Joe, Steve McQueen, Dowsing, In the Mall, Yes But So What, Cross Patch,* and *Goldberg Street.*]

Goldberg Street: Short Plays and Monologues. New York: Grove, 1985. [Contains *Goldberg Street, Cross Patch, Two Conversations, Two Scenes, The Spanish Prisoner, Yes But So What, Conversations with the Spirit World, Pint's a Pound the World Around, Dowsing, Deer Dogs, In the Mall, Maple Sugaring, Morris and Joe, The Dog, Film Crew, Four AM, The Power Outage, Food, Columbus Avenue, Steve McQueen, Yes, The Blue Hour: City Sketches, A Sermon, Shoeshine, Litko: a Dramatic Monologue, In Old Vermont,* and *All Men Are Whores: an Inquiry.*]

Reunion and *Dark Pony.* New York: Grove, 1979

Reunion, Dark Pony, The Sanctity of Marriage. New York: French, 1982

Sexual Perversity in Chicago and *Duck Variations.* New York: French, 1977; Grove, 1978.

The Shawl and *Prairie du Chien.* New York: Grove, 1985. London: Methuen, 1989.

Short Plays and Monologues. New York: Dramatists Play Service, 1981. [Contains *All Men Are Whores, The Blue Hour, In Old Vermont, Litko, Prairie du Chien, A Sermon,* and *Shoeshine.*]

Three Children's Plays. New York: Grove, 1986. [Contains *The Poet and the Rent, The Frog Prince,* and *The Revenge of the Space Pandas.*]

Three Jewish Plays. New York: French, 1987. [Contains *The Dis-appearance of the Jews, Goldberg Street*, and *The Luftmensch*.]
The Water Engine and *Mr. Happiness*. New York: Grove, 1978.
The Woods, Lakeboat, and *Edmond*. New York: Grove, 1987.

Collections of Essays

Writing in Restaurants. New York: Viking Penguin, 1986: London: Faber, 1988. [Collection of 30 essays written over ten years as newspaper and magazine articles, lectures, and catalogue introductions; including Mamet's reflections on aspects of the theatre (among them a moving tribute to Tennessee Williams and a stimulating critique of *The Cherry Orchard*), radio drama, working in Hollywood, the nature of fashion, the Oscar ceremonies, his passion for poker, the disappearance of the traditional pool-hall, and brief but witty glimpses of his family life.]
Some Freaks. New York: Viking Penguin, 1989; London: Faber, 1990. ['An extraordinary variety of subjects catches his attention, among them handguns, boxing, Disneyland, and the decor of Jewish homes. His value as an essayist is his knack of probing beneath the surface of seeming trivialities' (Christopher Lehmann-Haupt, *Image*, 4 Dec. 1989).]

Individual Articles and Essays

'Sad Comedy about Actors', *New York Times*, 16 Oct. 1977, Sec 2, p. 7.
'Playwrights on Resident Theaters: What Is to Be Done?' *Theater*, X (Summer 1979), p. 82.
'Final Cut: Special Delivery: David Mamet', *Cinema*, 6 March 1981.
'Mamet in Hollywood', *Horizon* , Nov. 1981, p. 56-7.
'Why I Write for Chicago Theatre', *Vanity Fair*, Nov. 1984.
'I Lost It at the Movies', *American Film*, XII (June 1987).
'Fighting Words', *Playboy*, Dec.1989.
'Cold Toast', *Condé Nast Traveller*, Nov. 1990.

Interviews

Witz, David, *Chicago Theater*, I, No. 1 (Feb. 1977).
Terry, Clifford, *Chicago Tribune*, 8 May 1977.
Dzielak, Steven, *New York Arts Journal*, Feb.-Mar. 1978.
Interview Magazine, March 1983. [Donald Sultan is a co-participant.]
Nuwer, Hank, 'Two Gentlemen of Chicago: David Mamet and Stuart Gordon', *South Carolina Review*, XVII (Spring 1985), p. 9-20.

Roudané, Matthew C., 'An Interview with David Mamet', *Studies in American Drama, 1945-Present*, I (1986), p. 73-81.

Savran, David, 'David Mamet', *In Their Own Words: Contemporary American Playwrights* (New York: Theatre Communications Group, 1988), p. 132-44. [Shortened version in *American Theatre*, IV, No. 6 (September 1987).]

Schvey, Henry I., 'Celebrating the Capacity for Self-Knowledge', *New Theatre Quarterly*, IV, No. 13 (February 1988).

b: Secondary Sources

Full-Length Studies

Bigsby, C. W. E., *David Mamet*. London: Methuen, 1985.

Carroll, Dennis, *David Mamet*. New York: St. Martin's, 1987.

Dean, Anne, *David Mamet: Language as Dramatic Action*. Rutherford: Fairleigh Dickinson University Press, 1990.

Major Articles and Chapters in Books

Gale, Steven H., 'David Mamet: the Plays, 1972-1980', *Essays on Contemporary American Drama*, ed. Hedwig Bock and Albert Wertheim (Munich: Hueber, 1981), p. 207-23.

Cohn, Ruby, 'Narrower Straits: Ribman, Rabe, Guare, Mamet', *New American Dramatists* (London: Macmillan, 1982), p. 41-6.

Bigsby, C. W. E., 'David Mamet', *A Critical Introduction to Twentieth-Century American Drama, Vol. 3: Beyond Broadway* (Cambridge University Press, 1985), p. 251-90.

Almani, Guido, 'David Mamet, a Virtuoso of Invective', *Critical Angles: European Views of Contemporary American Literature*, ed. Marc Chenetier (Carbondale: Southern Illinois University Press, 1986), p. 191-207, 241-2.

Demastes, William W., 'David Mamet's Dis-Integrating Drama', *Beyond Naturalism: a New Realism in American Theatre* (New York: Greenwood Press, 1988).

Bibliographies

Davis, J. Madison, and John Coleman, 'David Mamet: a Classified Bibliography', *Studies in American Drama, 1945-Present* (1986), p. 83-101. [Most comprehensive bibliography to date : primary bibliography includes 42 items (plays, screenplays, and essays); secondary bibliography lists more than 400 interviews, critical articles, reviews, and biographical essays, selected from American and Canadian scholarly and popular publications.]

Schlueter, June, 'David Mamet', *Contemporary Authors, Bibliography Series: American Dramatists* (Detroit: Gale Research, 1989), p. 141-169. [Primary and secondary bibliographies, with a sectionalized bilbiographical essay which includes commentary on bibliographies and checklists, interviews, and critical studies (books, major reviews, articles, and sections from books).]

Trigg, Joycelyn, 'David Mamet', *American Playwrights since 1945: a Guide to Scholarship, Criticism, and Performance*, ed. Philip C Kolin (Westport, Conn.: Greenwood Press, 1989), p. 259-88. [Primary bibliography includes notes on the production history of the plays. Survey of secondary sources includes bibliographies, biographies, influences, general studies, analyses of individual plays, and future research opportunities.]

Archival Resources

Goodman Theater Archives, Special Collections Division, Chicago Public Library. [Material relating to the Mamet/Mosher period: reviews, programmes, production notes, etc.]

St. Nicholas Theater Archives, Special Collections Division, Chicago Public Library. [Covers complete history of company, including reviews, programmes, production notes and budgets, prompt copies, and draft scripts.]

Billy Rose Theater Collection, Library of Performing Arts, Lincoln Center, New York. [Reviews, cuttings, photographs of American productions.]

Mamet Archive, Goldsmiths' College, University of London. [A research resource including details of all major productions in America, Europe, South Africa, Australia, and Japan, with reviews, programmes, posters, photographs, interviews, etc.]

TOFT (Theater on Film and Tape) Collection, Library of Performing Arts, Lincoln Center, New York. [Includes video cassettes of productions, as noted in Section 2, of *A Life in the Theatre*, *The Woods*, *The Water Engine*, *Reunion* and *Dark Pony*, *Edmond*, and *Glengarry Glen Ross*. Also scenes from the following: *Duck Variations* (as performed in *Emerging Playwrights*, 1977, including an interview with Mamet by Richard Barr); *Duck Variations* (as performed in *New Actors for the Classics*, 1980); *Sanford Meisner: the Theatre's Best Kept Secret* (Playhouse Repertory, New York, 1984).